THE TIGER'S HEART

By the Same Author

*

NOTES ON SOME FIGURES
BEHIND T. S. ELIOT

THE
TIGER'S HEART

EIGHT ESSAYS ON
SHAKESPEARE

By

Herbert Howarth

his Tygers hart wrapt in a Players hyde

NEW YORK

OXFORD UNIVERSITY PRESS

1970

Library of Congress Catalog Card Number: 70–106057

Printed in Great Britain
by R. and R. Clark Limited
Edinburgh

Acknowledgments

For permission to reprint four of these chapters, or parts of them, it is a pleasure to thank: W. J. Gage Ltd., Toronto, Canada, publishers of *Stratford Papers on Shakespeare 1961* (edited by Professor B. W. Jackson); Dr. James G. McManaway, editor of *Shakespeare Quarterly*; Dr. William E. Miller, editor of *The Library Chronicle*; and Professor Kenneth Muir, editor of *Shakespeare Survey*.

Contents

Shakespeare's Gentleness

AMBITION was a vice much practised, much condemned by the Tudors. Snobbery was and is a vice much practised and condemned. This is a story of vice and the extraordinary things a poet makes of his vices.

There is only one adjective in Ben Jonson's lines to the Reader of the First Folio: 'gentle' in the phrase 'gentle Shakespeare', which has become a byword. What did he mean by that solitary, and therefore telling, qualification? Possibly it was no more than a conventional expression of esteem. But the tribe of Ben liked obituaries in which a keyword characterized both the man and his style. When he himself was commemorated in the next decade, Falkland and Duppa called their volume *Jonsonus Virbius*.[1] 'Virbius' is, to be sure, as unusual as 'gentle' is usual; but they were dealing with a learned poet, and had to find a correspondingly learned word; and they used it to imply at once his learning, his two-man-size physique, and his literary ideal of chastity (of which the address *To the Reader*, refusing all adjectives but one, is an example). In the same comprehensive manner Jonson intended 'gentle' to recall Shakespeare's struggle to establish his father's gentle rank; to endorse the grant of the patent by the College of Arms; to recall the civil demeanour with which he attempted to impress his gentility on his acquaintance; and to record how the gentle style had first distinguished his writing from his rivals', and had remained his most supple strength.

I

In the Shakespearian tradition, 'gentle' has been detached from the style and has come down to us only as a description of the man, forming that household image in which he appears wise and sympathetic. The purpose of this chapter is to recover the history of an important Shakespearian style and to indicate its charm for an élite audience and its yet greater charm for the general audience. 'Gentle' is certainly associated with style in Jonson's more elaborate ode *To the Memory of my Beloved, the Author*; in the discovery of Shakespeare's 'brave notions, and gentle expressions'; and in the claim of Heminges and Condell that their dramatist 'as he was a happie imitator of Nature, was a most gentle expresser of it'.

Our dominant problems are those handed down by our fathers: their involuntary legacy of unfulfilled ambitions. Shakespeare's mother was a gentlewoman. His father had desired to be called a gentleman. John Shakespeare was one of those goodmen, so numerous according to the *Institucion of a Gentleman* of 1555,[2] who were seeking the higher status. He negotiated for a gentleman's coat-of-arms, and as long as he was prosperous had hopes of a result; his 'credit' was a point in his favour—he would be able to sustain the rank if it were conceded. The mood in the Stratford home when Shakespeare could first understand his parents' talk was probably ebullient; he must have received the impression that the grant of the coat-of-arms was imminent and that it was merited. Instead there followed the depression of his father's fortunes, and he grew up in the lean years, with the natural consequences that he determined to be prosperous, never to have to bear domestic

hardship again, and that he set a high valuation on the
unachieved coat-of-arms and the status it represented.
He wanted to secure the coat-of-arms for his father as
a consolation in old age, and he wanted the title to reflect on himself and prove him 'William Shakespeare,
gentleman'.

Prosperity was the first objective; and it had to be
prosperity rather than mere sufficiency, for, as Hotson
has remarked,[3] securing a patent was an expensive
affair. It is part of the paradox of the Shakespearian,
and of the human, situation, that in order to become,
what he was sure he deserved to be, Shakespeare the
gentleman, he had also to become Shakespeare the
business-man, and a part of him was so exhilarated by
the management of money that he remained Shakespeare the (sometimes ungentle) business-man long
after the pressure of necessity had relaxed. On his
dramatic method the first effect of his problem was that
he learned, with speed, to cultivate the box-office. He
fed into his plays those pieces of deliberate showmanship which gratified and multiplied the crowds: pieces
of pageantry and spectacle; quasi-legendary episodes of
history; a masque; pieces of pathos, Blanche deciding
between husband and family,[4] Arthur pleading for his
eyes.[5] In fact one or two early plays are careless of
overall structure, and they go forward or turn course
as Shakespeare sees opportunities for strokes that will
please the crowd, whether or not scene be consistent
with scene. Later he learned to integrate the wilfully
popular scenes with the evolution of a play's question;
part of his strength was to succeed in his errors, not to
abandon them but to find purposes for them. And his

common touch was as excellent as his gentleness. I am not for a moment decrying his capture of the public, nor the inventiveness, simplicity, and ultimately the proportion of the strokes of showmanship; his assault on the box-office was, in the strictest sense, *crafty*. But in the early days in the theatre he probably himself classified these clever passages as something apart from, even hostile to, the voice in him which was practising the language of a gentleman. Although the working-out of a problem always gives a poet pleasure, and to that extent he enjoyed their execution, he thought of them as an intermediate step to economic success, and of that as an intermediate step to social recognition.

A man seeking a favour in Elizabethan London, whose motions we can best understand if we think of it in terms of an oriental city, needed something else besides money: the support of friends. Shakespeare found himself requiring not merely the patron-in-general that every poet wanted, but a protector who could shorten his lobbying with the College of Arms. This is the situation that lies behind *Venus and Adonis*. Shakespeare looked round for a promising quarry, and found him in Southampton: young, attractive, and, best of all, close to the court favourite, Essex. But the interest of Southampton and his group could not, he fancied, be gained by box-office techniques. He must write a courtier's poem, a poem of dazzling elegance. Particularly, since he desired support in the application for the gentleman's crest, he must write a poem that manifested him a gentleman. *Venus and Adonis* is a deliberate first display of the gentle style.

If a test of beauty is 'fitness for purpose', *Venus* is a

beautiful poem. To prove its writer the master-poet it demonstrates every weapon in the Renaissance poet's equipment. It offers to equal Ovid in English, by providing an English *Metamorphoses*, and does so with such triumph that the cry goes up 'The English Ovid!'[6] It proves its writer a gentleman by the ease of its brilliance, the disinvolvement, the *sprezzatura*. Addressed to young men, it must be wanton; but addressed by a gentleman to noblemen, it must be free from crudity; and it is both, by dint of a technique of transposition, the attachment of the erotic words not to the protagonist but to the landscape, the wild boar, the undergrowth:

> Some catch her by the neck, some kiss her face,
> Some twine about her thigh to make her stay.[7]

It will tantalize, even dismay, any reader who does not love rhetoric as well as concupiscence. It exhibits the arts of soft appeal, of severe reply, of distinctions well-focused, of proverbs well-placed, of uncommon fancies and vivid pictures from common life. It makes poetry of the gentleman's occupations: his hunting, horses, coursing, and discoursing. Above all, it exhibits the art of discourse. When young men like Valentine and Proteus and Southampton went to court, they expected to hear sweet discourse and to learn the skill of it.[8] *Venus and Adonis* is a display of discourse to enchant the ear. In the closing stanzas of the poem Shakespeare extends his resources to the utmost:

> 'Poor flower', quoth she, 'this was thy father's
>   guise—
> Sweet issue of a more-sweet-smelling sire—
> For every little grief to wet his eyes:
> To grow unto himself was his desire,

And so 'tis thine; but know, it is as good
To wither in my breast as in his blood.

'Here was thy father's bed, here in my breast;
Thou are the next of blood, and 'tis thy right:
Lo, in this hollow cradle take thy rest,
My throbbing heart shall rock thee day and
    night . . .'[9]

He tells of gifts descended from father to son but in the
voice of a mother-and-lover whose son has perished and
will never use the gifts. An amazing intervention of his
personal problem at the moment of the supreme effort
—an effort in which masculine gentleness turns into
pathos, a form of feminine gentleness.

While Shakespeare was apparently interested only
in the gentle side of his lineage, he owed a great deal to
the combination in him of the gentle and the yeoman
strains: owed his energy to it, and his success. He succeeded in most things that he attempted (except the
handing-down of his name and the prized coat-of-arms
through the male line; that was life's Greek revenge).
Certainly he succeeded with *Venus and Adonis*. We
know he obtained Southampton's attention, because
the 'graver' *Lucrece* followed,[10] according to promise.
And is it not significant that the date of the first draft of
the College of Arms award to John Shakespeare is
20 October 1596,[11] when Essex' popularity was at its
height after the fun at Cadiz?[12] Shakespeare, the actor,
knew the art of timing, and he pressed his noble friend
to press *his* noble friend for a decisive word at the ideal
moment.

Is there an equivalent to *Venus* in the theatre? There
is a sudden, plenitudinous exhibition of the gentle style

in *A Midsummer Night's Dream*, and I suspect, while admitting the tangles of the dating problem, that in this comedy Shakespeare exhilaratedly converted the art of the Latin *Metamorphoses* and the English *Venus and Adonis* into theatrical terms. Requiring inventions as brilliant as those in *Venus*, but *dramatic* inventions, he concocts a plot and characters to allegorize the metamorphosis of English literature in his time. In his time and through him, and not least through this play that tells about it, the literature grown in the native sand during the middle ages wed the neo-classical literature which had lately immigrated from the warm south. We are told, in the voice of a wife's complaint of infidelity, that poetry has stolen away from fairyland to live the Theocritan idyll

> Playing on pipes of corn and versing love
> To amorous Phillida[13]

and that had been the frequent truancy of Shakespeare's sixteenth-century predecessors, but now the very poetry that makes the complaint is both the poetry of the Italian flute and the poetry of mediaeval fairyland. We know Ovid's star is over the play from the name Titania,[14] from the metamorphosis of Bottom, and from this major metamorphosis of our literature which the play dreams. The poetry, with a range of styles which the poet enjoys switching and commanding, is impeccably gentle in the courtier's sense when courtiers are the speakers, and gentle in the sense of easy and brilliant in the fairy scenes. In the class of brilliant fancy there is no poetry lovelier than the calendar of the freak seasons

> hoary-headed frosts
> Fall in the fresh lap of the crimson rose,

And on old Hiems' thin and icy crown
An odorous chaplet of sweet summer buds
Is, as in mockery, set. . . .[15]

Look at that from one angle and it is Ovid in English;
look at it from another, and it is no such thing but
mediaeval personification; and in fact it is a marriage of
the two. And the blent poetry has that easy and delighted carriage that was the signature of *Venus and
Adonis*; it is only more delighted, more mobile and easy.
The lines are warm—and even the frosts!—with the
pleasure of the new adept in managing his art.

For all its success, there is a lamentable contradiction
in the early gentle style: the style is *exhibited*; and it is
not permissible for a gentleman to exhibit.[16] The English image of the gentleman and his gentleness is closely
related to the national practice of understatement (and
to the morality, which perhaps grows out of it, of doing
good by stealth). Though Shakespeare revelled in his
first manner, he soon saw that it would not do. He
dropped the ostentation and worked his way towards a
deeper gentleness.

He found it in the plays of his 'early middle' period.
Here he has passed from the brilliance of courtliness to
the charity of courtesy. As occasion serves, he makes a
character speak with modesty, good will, mercy, kindness, in words that could not be more telling yet could
not be less ostentatious. Sometimes the gentleness lies
precisely in that check on ostentation or power, that
conscious moderation. Like the words, the music of the
style betokens power controlled, though also sweetness
of disposition. I will quote two instances from *The
Merchant of Venice*. Bassanio, just now conqueror of

Portia's hand and her estate, and therefore already entitled to welcome guests in her home, uses his title; but the moment he has spoken he detects in himself an unmannerly haste, and gently moderates his pretensions:

> Lorenzo and Salerio, welcome hither;
> If that the youth of my new interest here
> Have power to bid you welcome. By your leave,
> I bid my very friends and countrymen,
> Sweet Portia, welcome.[17]

If ever we attempt this kind of modest self-correction in our private talk, we may have to do it by using the pattern Shakespeare has struck here: the recapitulation of our rash statement in qualified terms. A little later in the same scene Bassanio uses the same tone of modesty, and a similar structure of repetition and qualification, though this time his gentleness is that he is confessing faults while claiming an essential innocence at their heart. For love's sake, he says, he has concealed his debts:

> Gentle lady,
> When I did first impart my love to you,
> I freely told you, all the wealth I had
> Ran in my veins, I was a gentleman;
> And then I told you true; and yet, dear lady,
> Rating myself at nothing, you shall see
> How much I was a braggart. . . .[18]

With these gentle, chastened locutions, and the winsome compliments into which they often grow, Shakespeare captivated his audiences. The noblemen could, if vain, flatter themselves that they were faithfully reflected; if wise, appreciate a felicity beyond their own. And what about the general spectator? Castiglione had swept England just before Shakespeare was born,[19] and for fifty years there was a national craving, permeating all classes but especially the less privileged, to speak with the grace of the courtier (whose style, thought Sidney,[20] was the soundest style). Eager to educate himself in a pleasing diction, the general spectator was glad to take his lessons from the stage. Shakespeare's plays were the three-dimensional Courtesy-Books of Everyman.

Perhaps there was an additional reason for the popularity of this style. Perhaps the secret of the English attitude to art is a reverence for moral music; when the English hear morality and music in indissoluble fusion, they are struck to silence, overwhelmed. Of course they love the immoral and amoral too, but then they are conscious that they are adventuring, and part of their joy is the joy of the margin, the perilous brink. Shakespeare's gentleness of the deeper second variety is a moral music right at the centre of the English experience. He had come to it as the result of the refinement of the first literature of his social ambitions by his growing sensibility. Now, as he heard the audiences sigh with pleasure at it, he recognized, astonished perhaps by the revelation, that it was even more beneficial to the box-office than those pieces of showmanship with which he had first wooed the crowd.

Had Shakespeare been a complacent man, he might have continued to the end of his life writing gentle lines for the profit and the satisfaction of watching them score their effect on the audience. But he was an experimenter; and his world-picture was changing. A new intention can be traced in *Much Ado about Nothing*. He

has designed the play in two parts: in the first Don
Pedro is the pattern of gentleness; in the second, victimized by malpractice, he allows himself to swerve
from it. He is gentleness pre-eminent when Beatrice
cries heigh-ho for a husband. 'Lady Beatrice, I will
get you one', he offers. And she, in her madcap pert-
ness:

> I would rather have one of your father's getting. Hath your
> grace ne'er a brother like you? Your father got excellent
> husbands, if a maid could come by them.[21]

That is asking for a princely husband, and with another
prince it might be asking for a royal rebuff. But Shakespeare's view is that royalty does not rebuff, and Don
Pedro accepts the petition with the utmost charm: 'Will
you have me, lady?' and Beatrice, who realizes that her
wit went too far, comes back with the proper light-
hearted refusal, followed by a modest apology, which
the Don again turns with courtesy. But after the scene
at the window the Don thinks his friend wronged and
holds himself responsible, and gives himself to the
atrociously ungentle plan to repudiate Hero at the altar.
Hardin Craig has told us not to be offended, because
Hero was, to all appearances, violating the sacrament
of marriage by coming to it stained, and Shakespeare's
audience would consider Claudio justified. I would
crawl on my knees from Pennsylvania to Missouri to
listen to Hardin Craig, but I think that here,[22] as in his
whole conception of representing Shakespeare as the
vehicle of Renaissance norms, he eliminates half the
drama. Shakespeare was not a conformist; he was an
inquisitive man who, as Hardin Craig has elsewhere so
well observed, likes to balance the pros and cons of a

question. Hardin Craig justifies Claudio, but Beatrice does not:

> What, bear her in hand until they come to take hands; and then, with public accusation, uncovered slander, unmitigated rancour,–O God, that I were a man! I would eat his heart in the market-place.[23]

Of the operation in 'unmitigated rancour' of the Latin word for 'gentle' Shakespeare would be more aware than we can be. Gentleness has been worsted; and through Beatrice's anger–and she, though a madcap, is never guilty of wrong feeling–Shakespeare says that he does not like its defeat, does not like Claudio's conformist retaliation against Hero. Ah, what a hero *he* had been, if he had continued patient and the Don gentle. (But Shakespeare does not lay down a definite ruling. For an objective of his art by this time is to set his audience arguing the unresolved question: to have them carry the play with them to the tavern or to bed, not in print, of course, but in their warring souls and on their tongues. How good to have housewives and apprentices protracting the play in their memories as they debate who was right: Claudio or Beatrice? *Hamlet* was Shakespeare's longest-lived success in the set-them-talking vein. But *Much Ado* was a keen contemporary success.)

In Shakespeare's middle work there is a gradual merging of his intellectual curiosity and his 'gentleness'. At the beginning they were separate because 'gentleness' was bound up with his ambition, was an instrument ruthlessly handled for the furthering of his ambition. He had wanted money, women, noble friends, success, and prestige. By 1599 he was established in prestige and property; he had been recognized as poet and dramatist; he had enjoyed women in sufficiency, or as much sufficiency as ever contents a man; he had met the noble and powerful, and now wished no more of them. So his ambitions had been either realized or had been let go in repletion. He did not have to exploit a skill for ambition's sake. He was liberated from an unpleasant paradox: the ruthlessness of gentleness. 'Gentleness' remained, free of the purposes of ambition, and developed as his sympathetic insight into human beings developed. He grew gentler because he was interested in the human problem, and he became the more engaged with the human problem, and more subtle and discerning in his treatment of his characters, because he was gentle.

An experimenter gives his special interest to new tools whose resources he has not yet fully explored. At the very period, 1594 to 1599, when he was most exploiting gentleness as his best stock-in-trade, he began to develop, as if by an inner protest, non-gentle energies. He remembered a very early, crude sketch of non-gentle energy, the Bastard, and built him into Hotspur. Hotspur is energy naked, energy that rejects the insulation of gentleness, energy that rejects gentle poetry and offers in contrast a poetry with the harsh metallic ring of real life. So strong was Shakespeare's intuition of an alternative to his current mask of gentleness, that it billowed out, in the same play, into Falstaff and his cronies. Shakespeare first drew them, as he thought, in dislike, weaving them coarsely from recollections of the antisocial impulses of his youth and observation of the contemporary footloose, factious younger sons whom Trevor-Roper has described in *The Gentry 1540–1640*.

He created them in dislike, but that Anti-Man in his stomach still sympathized with them and insisted on a value, perhaps the power of the vulgar hold on life, in them. And he found that his audiences, regardless of their fashionable Courtiering, detected his unconscious sympathy and shared it and responded to it and loved what he had devised in contempt.

So by 1600 his success was multifarious. He had much to busy himself with besides courtesy. Especially he had to take account of his own reaction to his multifarious success. He found, as Eliot has found, that 'fools' approval stings', and that the sting itself is an incentive to new writing. So came the work which was foreshadowed in the fourth act of *Much Ado*.

The new writing made its powerful impact—and created its own new success—by censuring the world in which he had succeeded, censuring himself, too, for the means of his success. He felt that in winning prestige, prosperity and status, he had exploited beauty and refinement as a mere instrument of ambition. Honesty had been transformed into a bawd. He discerned such indignity in himself that it were 'better my mother had not borne me'.[24] His subject became the imperfection of man, the shortfall from ideals, the disorder of society. In *Hamlet* grace and reason are jangled. In *Othello* the mildness that complements a soldier's courage is baffled and his sword turned from the heathen against a wife who is the very emblem of mildness. In *Julius Caesar* gentleness is wrested awry, the gentleness of Brutus. In *Troilus* gentleness has gone awry. Hector is the figuration of heroic gentleness—strength tempered by mercy, honour tempered by reason, reason

tempered by fellowship. But the world is so disjointed
that this great gentleness fails. We are told at the outset
of the play that it has broken down: 'He chid Andromache and struck his armourer'.[25] On the verge of the
final disaster we have to witness the repetition of its
symptomatic breaking. Andromache beseeches

> When was my lord so much ungently temper'd,
> To stop his ears against admonishment?[26]

but Hector is offended and offends and drives Andromache away while Cassandra wails his doom, his sun
setting in mass brutality, and debonair Troy sinking,
and the old chivalric code of courtesy and courageous
benignity ending. In these dramas of the human shortfall Shakespeare worked best and most often with
gentleness, because gentleness was the ideal he and his
age valued most. And above all he worked with it because
he had fallen short of it in the very act of becoming a
gentleman and a gentle poet; to exploit it was to fall short
of it, to succeed by it and in it was to contaminate it.

Shakespeare was the recipient of a long tradition,
which hoped that the hereditary aristocrat would represent the high virtues of his ancestors but knew that
he might not; knew too that the aristocratic virtues
might appear in a man of another class; and maintained
that the virtues, as fulfilled in deeds, must always be
preferred to the mere title. He was a dangerous writer
to assume responsibility for the tradition, for he did
overvalue the hereditary element. But he came, in the
second half of his career, to make two studies of a bad
aristocrat and the failure of a strain. The first and obvious case is *All's Well that Ends Well*. Son of a nobleman
who was a pattern for the courtesy-books and of a

mother as wise and generous as she is grand, Bertram is—except for vigour in war—empty of the virtues. Shakespeare mixes the condemnation of Bertram the bad son with his condemnation of Bertram the hollow young man among young men all hollow. Bertram is, probably, the first indication in the plays that the dramatist has crossed a threshold: identifies with the ageing; feels his difference from the latest entrants into the arena where men fight the game of life; is irritated, and betrays his irritation, with the young. In some measure this consideration—that he is angry with all young men, not only with the bad aristocrat—modifies the force of the complaint that the gentle powers do not always descend down the blood from father to child. But the criticism of the hereditary principle *is* there. At the very moment when he has begun to close his mind to the new generation, Shakespeare has begun to open his mind and see beyond some of his most impelling daydreams. He invents a new pattern of decency, Lafeu. Lafeu is not gentle. He is plain and to the point; hard; and yet humane. Lafeu writes himself 'man'.[27] A few years earlier Shakespeare had wanted above all to write himself 'gentleman', and had thought it the crown of his efforts when he did so.

The second case is *Coriolanus*. The tragedy of a simple man, it is deliberately complex. Here is a play which is a study in the aristocratic mind, a study written from the standpoint of 'the right-hand file',[28] 'the honour'd number'.[29] We see Rome from the patrician palace; when the crowd murmurs we are made to listen with patrician ears; we make war from the general's knoll. Yet, apparently a rightist play, it is a disclosure from within of the truths about the right. An aristocrat may have one or other of the virtues of his race. He never has the ideal composition of the virtues for which he is sung. He may love Rome: Volumnia loves Rome, but she does not love the people. He may have a sense of compromise, like Menenius, who talks the crowd fair, but only as an astute temporizer, not out of sympathy. He may love war, like Martius, who has the war-god's name, without loving anything else. Flickers of chivalry in these knights of Rome when they are on the battlefield: the selfless esteem of Cominius for the better soldier at his side; Martius' admirable rejection of the booty, and his admirable—but imperfect and quickly-let-go—plea for mercy for the poor man who once sheltered him at Corioli.[30] Off the field the light is extinct. In Martius there is no gentleness. And the lack of it is strikingly dramatized: his voice is ungentle: he never (unless at the crucial moment of the crucial scene in which he overcomes himself and spares the City) uses the quiet tones which are the sign of an inner, many-faceted gentleness. The play is a concerto for percussion. Shakespeare has a habit of telling us through the comments of other characters how he intends a rôle to be played; and he is perfectly clear in his directions for Martius:

> with thy grim looks and
> The thunder-like percussion of thy sounds,
> Thou madest thine enemies shake, as if the world
> Were feverous and did tremble[31]

and

> The shepherd knows not thunder from a tabor
> More than I know the sounds of Martius' tongue
> From every meaner man[32]

The insistent thunder is part of the energy of the warrior, part of the horror of the man. It is the corollary of his son's mammocking of a butterfly. The image of the smashed butterfly[33]—the fragilities of life smashed, the psyche smashed—runs through the play to illustrate the strength that only mutilates, and station without grace. Power and percussion are fine in a man but only at the right time and only as the complement of sweetness, light, restraint.

The best man, the pure Orlando, laid aside his strength:[34] let gentleness my strong enforcement be. That was Shakespeare in a gay mood, playing with the story of the dispossessed who yet has all the charms that came down with his blood. When a hostile world seems to deny his rights he goes to the Forest of Arden, his mother's womb, and is taken into the timeless confusions of a dream, out of which grows a harmony: whereupon the world accepts him and grants his gifts their scope. But *Coriolanus*, nine years later, is written in a very different mood. Sombre and realist. It is a study induced by the burial of Mary Arden on September 9, 1608. That powerful woman had perhaps, like Thomas Hardy's wife, been in the habit of telling her husband, 'Never forget that you married a lady'. Now her son buried her and reflected on the tenacity with which a mother forms her son: how she imposes her standards and can hardly fail to win; yet her very victory may be disaster for the son, because it is *her* victory. He understood the meaning of Achilles' heel: the mother who dips her son in immortalizing fluid must leave him vulnerable at the point where her hand held and protected him. A mother teaches and prepares

her son, but there will always be something she has forgotten to teach, and without which the rest collapses.
Volumnia taught Martius war-passion and wound-
courage, assuming that a self-effacing love of the City
would inevitably come with these virtues. It did not. At
last she demonstrated the paramount claims of the City
by sacrificing her son to save it. And he accepted her
demonstration and acquiesced in the sacrifice: 'Most
dangerously you have with him prevail'd'.[35] *Coriolanus*
is a beautiful exhibition of the tragic choice, in which
every decision is fatal, though one nobler than another.
Martius can only rise above the mother-formed,
mother-warped destroyer and be free of his old infantile
self by letting his mother exert her will on him once
more. And she, if she elevates him, also destroys him
by the exertion. The most cruelly ironic scene in
Shakespeare is only seven lines long: the fifth scene of
the last act of *Coriolanus* when Volumnia passes back
through the City gates cheered and garlanded by the
crowds: 'our patroness, the life of Rome!'

Unshout the shout that banish'd Martius,
Repeal him with the welcome of his mother . . .[36]

Across the political study of the aristocracy Shakespeare has drawn the psychological study of demanding
mother and obedient son, which is also a study of the
process of handing down the aristocratic values by
indoctrination.

In the last plays Shakespeare moves erratically—but it
may be that this word should be *freely*, because he is
now detached from the problem—between the view that
gentleness incorruptibly descends down the blood-
stream from parent to child and the view that descent

does not matter until endorsed by deeds. 'Good wombs have borne bad sons',[37] says Miranda. In the long and fulsome peroration of *Henry VIII* with which Cranmer prophesies the days of Elizabeth, it is promised as one of the felicities of her reign that

> those about her
> From her shall read the perfect ways of honour,
> And by those claim their greatness, not by blood.[38]

But the innate aristocracy of Marina, Perdita, and Miranda is an argument for the blood. Spying Polixenes, it will be remembered, tries to trap Perdita into a confession that she hopes for a marriage to a Prince far above her: surely she likes gillyflowers:

> You see, sweet maid, we marry
> A gentler scion to the wildest stock,
> And make conceive a bark of baser kind
> By bud of nobler race; this is an art
> Which does mend nature, change it rather, but
> The art itself is nature.[39]

A point proper to Shakespeare the son of a mixed marriage, and proper to the retired Shakespeare occupied with his garden; and too nice a point for Polixenes' unfriendly purpose. But though Perdita can't find an answer to it, her royal nature, says Shakespeare reverting to his sometime deference, rejects it:

> I'll not put
> The dibble in earth to set one slip of them;
> No more than were I painted I would wish
> This youth should say 'twere well and only
>   therefore
> Desire to breed by me.

One must not sanctify the last plays or the man who wrote them. Polixenes' trap witnesses that at the end there still remained in Shakespeare, amid the clear-seeing, an inexpungable nucleus of that Proustian snobbery with which he started his work; and still, as in the earlier years, Shakespeare metamorphosed that besetting vice into literature.

It matches the terms of the pardon he offers the world, that this contradiction still remained with him. Hypersensitively aware of the partnership of folly and merit (in Wolsey or you or me or himself), of dream and reality, of violence and gentleness, he implies that the beauty of life is the collision of opposites—and the beauty of art the collation of opposites. So he startlingly uses violence and tenderness in the last scenes of *Pericles* and *Cymbeline*. At the climax of *Pericles* he just failed—supposing our text is correct—in mating violence and tenderness to the illumination of each. The story lent him a perfect opportunity: Pericles struck his un-known daughter before he was united with her. It looks from the text as if Shakespeare could not make up his mind how far to take this situation, so near to his personal difficulties as a father who loved his daughters and suffered from his love. Should he do as he had sometimes done in the past, refine the plot and avoid a shock which might be too painful to the sensibility? Or should he admit the pain which is inseparable from the transport of love? Torn between the two solutions, he blurred the issue. That 'something that glows'[40] upon her cheek appears to be Marina's instinct, not his passionate blow; the violence he does her is not an outright blow but a crazy shaking and a thrust away. The scene has its tenderness, but its most penetrating dramatic possibility has been muffed. Not so with *Cymbeline*.

Here he does not flinch. In the superb 'long take' of
the last scene Posthumus strikes the unrecognized
Imogen.[41] That is a blow to break the heart of the
striker, and by the mystery of love it is the completion
of love. It is also the completion of a Shakespearian
process: the refiner of English drama has become its
brutalizer, but in accepting the toughness of the world
he has mastered its purest and most ecstatic gentleness.

And he has forgiven himself. He has even forgiven
himself for writing plays. Polixenes adjures Camillo

> As you are certainly a gentleman, thereto
> Clerk-like experienced, which no less adorns
> Our gentry than our parents' noble names . . .[42]

Shakespeare's clerk-like experience was his theatre, and
he now accepted it, including the plays of gentleness
and the plays of protest, as an embellishment of his
gentility.

I promised to consider biography a little, but style
mainly, and I do not want to finish this chapter in terms
of Weltanschauung. My last point shall rather be one
of theatrical technique, the effect of Shakespeare's concern for the gentle style on the actors of his company.
We gather from *Hamlet* that he deplored the railing he
found habitual among the actors.[43] And obviously a
practitioner of the gentle style would deplore it: his
gentle lines would lose their character if they were
bombasted. So he urged restraint in elocution and gesture. His suggestions must gradually have trained his
company in the command of lower pitches; that in turn
must have given more value to ranting when ranting
was apposite; and the men must have realized the advantages of a range of light and shade, and have worked

to increase it. Thus Shakespeare improved the instrument for which he wrote; and as he heard it improving, he could extend himself further and write lines which challenged the actors to new subtleties of pitch and texture. At length he could write *Antony and Cleopatra*, which is virtuoso scoring for a human orchestra, demanding swift and brilliant shifts of elocution, and culminating, when the queen and her girls put serpents to the nipple, in a texture of sound, ravishing, orgasmic, bizarre, that no poet had previously known how to ask from his players. And he could characterize and criticize Coriolanus as a roaring voice because he could depend on the company to furnish a background of balances and contrasts. These were technical rewards for the once ambitious and self-indulgent cultivation of gentleness for gentility's sake.

The Early 1590's and the Changes of Heroick Song

It is well known how the poets of the early 1590's commented exultantly on their period. 'Loe now of English poesie comes the spring'—so the anonymous sonneteer,[1] who begs Henry Constable to return from exile and play his part in the new writing. Spenser, visiting the court to read *The Faerie Queene*, finds his monarch ringed by poets,[2] than whom

> ... better shepheards be not under skie,
> Nor better hable, when they list to blow
> Their pipes aloud, her name to glorifie.

London is thronged by new poets, 'Apollo's musical birds'.[3]

The best diminishes the appeal of the good, and the reader of literature thinks of the early 1590's as less attractive than the late 1590's, that tide of Shakespeare's most perfectly balanced plays, or the decade 1600–1610 in which masterpiece follows masterpiece. Yet the early period is quite as astonishing as its poets claimed. It is profuse not only in vernal improvisations but in finished art. Spenser publishes the first three books of *The Faerie Queene*, writes the next three, executes brilliant short pieces: and with each performance teaches his country the technique of musical architecture. The posthumous works of Sidney are published, setting the pattern in English for the prose-poetry medley (the fact that later writers failed to build on the pattern detracts nothing from his achievement), the sonnet sequence, and the prose of critical persuasion. Marlowe completes his work. Shakespeare completes a third of his work. If Shakespeare had died in 1596, that third would still be a major segment of English literature. It demonstrates his art of comedy, a unique arabesque of contrapuntal plots, contrapuntal tones, varied levels of poetry, prose, and song. It includes plays which do the most potent work of which literature is capable: introduce new figures into the world's imagination, figures which represent obscure reaches of the psyche, figures vital enough to lend themselves to the daily lives of every man and to examination and elaboration by creative minds in later epochs. *A Midsummer Night's Dream* and *Romeo and Juliet* are myth-making plays of that order; so in a lighter degree is *The Taming of the Shrew*.

The factors that coalesced to ripen the sudden literature were European developments in their specifically twisted English versions. Foremost, as we always say, was the revival of the classics, which suggested a grand image of man, but which also produced its warring antibody, the image of man as beast. In England, the Alaska of Europe, slow and moody in its distance and damp, the neo-classical pride in man and the hankering for southern luxuriance were bitterly combated by the pleasure-resistant puritanism of men like Yorkshire Ascham, and in the arts the struggle produced strange hybrid metaphors, strange tonalities ingeniously ambivalent. Throughout western Europe new schools and a new pedagogy released hitherto untapped energies. The extension of English education in 1500–1520 helped to produce the literature of 1590–1640, much as the Victorian Education Acts have elicited the angry writers from D. H. Lawrence to John Osborne. Throughout western Europe the geographical horizons were lifted by exploits which attested man's dynamism, and the consequent influx of wealth hastened shifts in the class structure and increased the opportunities for a busy leisure. England responded to the mystique of the horizons, but entered late, and too late, into the exploration of the western tropics, and in the endeavour to catch up invested piracy with a halo of virtue. Spain at last turned in retaliation to extinguish her small opponent; and because the opponent was a David against a Goliath the usurped name of virtue became legitimate, and the repulse of the Armada filled England with the delight of heroism and nationhood.

To this last event has often been attributed the rush of writing after 1588, especially as so much of the writing draws on English history and the word 'heroic' echoes through it. I have no wish to deny the national self-awareness. My intention in this paper is to affirm its presence, but to affirm, too, some peculiar features in it. It is not simple. The Bastard's loud rebuff, at the end of *King John*, to the three corners of the world, and Gaunt's dying vision of his little isle, are sometimes taken as the type of the patriotism of the time. I will suggest that they are exceptional rather than typical. When writers get hold of an ideal, they seldom treat it simply. There is a continuity in the attitudes of the English writers from the Elizabethans to the present day; and a typical and chronic English contrariness, by which in one school the real is abnegated for the ideal and in another the ideal critically and self-critically refused for the real, is already discernible in the Tudor analysis of England and heroism.

The heroic standard and the cultivation of epic by the 1590 poets were a legacy of a man who died two years before the Armada and 'the Yeare of Wonder': Philip Sidney. In the *Apology for Poetry* Sidney summons the categories of poetry before his reader in ascending order of importance. Last of them, and therefore at the apex of the art, is the 'Heroicall'.[4] His examples show that he is speaking of the epic. He goes on to indicate that the epic thrives only in a country which is living epically, fulfilling herself in active endeavour, of which war may, perhaps must, be a part. Don't let us take this as the common opinion of his time. There were people to whom it was obvious error. Gascoigne had already written *Dulce Bellum Inexpertis* on the gritty foundation of his Netherlands soldiering. To understand the matter we have to see Sidney amid his personal problems. In his richly-furnished mind there was a centre of melancholy. Almost as perfect as imperfect man can be, he could not tolerate human imperfection, could not rest content with himself or accept the faltering and paltering terms of existence. We may suspect that Shakespeare disinterred some elements of his character for Hamlet. He loathed, like every sensitive sixteenth-century man, the taint of the Court. Turning from the uncleanliness of the coulisses, he imagined a higher fulfilment in patriotic enterprise and heroic action: something out of Homer or Ennius. He must have talked the doctrine of the satisfying heroic life and of the art that should both urge it and reflect it in the years immediately preceding and following the *Apology*.

Spenser was talking with Sidney in 1579. Out of the conversations of the 'Areopagus'[5] came Spenser's decision to write *The Faerie Queene*. It would supply the lacuna that Sidney deplored, would be the missing epic, England's 'heroicall' poem. For his source he turned to the Arthurian tales. Significantly, he does not appear to have thought of the chroniclers. Real England was not heroical enough for him. The ascent of a Welsh Tudor to the throne had given a renewed royal aura to the Arthurian legends, which made it proper flattery to choose them; and, better than that for a poet attempting a poem to reach and represent the nation, the legends were the popular reading of the day; there was a tide of popular emotion running with them, and he could coast on it. On the other hand, there was an ideological difficulty attached to his choice. He was Protestant and academic; and the Protestant academics who had tutored him (and who had tutored Sidney) had reviled the Arthuriad for its 'Papistry' and bold bawdry. The artist in him overcame the sectarian and permitted him the choice for its spacious advantages. But the sectarian hastened after the artist, for he transformed his material to the Protestant and the moral. In the result *The Faerie Queene* is 'heroic' in two senses. The one is external and familiar: it is a narrative of 'Fierce warrs'. In this respect it meets Sidney's requirement, incites men to emulous action, promises them sanity and grace if they quest and endure and suffer wounds for a cause. The other is internal and higher. The heroic feats are allegorical. They incite men to an inner heroism, of which the outer is only a dream symbol: a resolute struggle towards holiness, chastity, prudence, the difficult virtues.

Dr. Hotson, for reasons of his own, has urged[6] that whenever the men of 1590 spoke of heroism they always understood a great deal more than military valour. He has gathered passages from J. Bossewell, Sir W. Alexander, John Ross, and Spenser himself to support the claim. I will quote the first, since it is the fullest. It is a list of 'Preceptes Heroical':

> . . . worship God. Honour the King. Obey the lawes. Be merciful. Desire honour and glorye for vertue . . . Perfourme what so ever thou promisest.

It is a noble passage, and so are the other three. But I cannot quite think with Dr. Hotson that they prove that an Elizabethan automatically thought of all these virtues when he heard the word 'hero'. They are not so much definitive as hortatory. They assume that there is an initial definition of hero, much simpler, less noble: the strong man who dares and does. They urge him to develop beyond the primitive definition. They invite him to discriminate: to dare and do only what is finest. They try to elevate the hero to the gentleman. This has long been the effort of society, intense because civilization depends on its success, and the more intense because success is rare. The Arthurian story is one of the most remarkable examples of the effort (we can only be surprised that Ascham and Baxter and the other divines ignored this side of the legends), and Spenser's task of moralizing his song was in one respect easy: he had only to elicit, enhance, augment what was already there. What we can say, on the hint of Dr. Hotson's citations taken together with the whole tendency of *The Faerie Queene*, is that the late years of the sixteenth century see a renewed drive in civilizing exhortation, and that the concept of the hero is a spearhead. The 'gentleman' in the Courtly sense is bidden be more of a hero, to *exert* himself for civilization; and the hero is encouraged to be more a gentleman, to control, subdue, direct his strength for civilization. This is true of the idealizing works of the epoch.

For *The Faerie Queene* is an act of idealization. If Sidney had lived to read it, would he have recognized, one wonders, how, by assimilating his dream of a military campaign into the old chivalric metaphor of the armed and questing knight, it at once criticized his ambition, which was captived to the truth of a foolish world, and evoked a truer ambition pointing him and every gentleman to the steeps of the seventh hill? *The Faerie Queene* sublimates Sidney. It is a sublime version of the Renaissance image of human grandeur in collision with the counter-image of human bestiality; and the grandeur prevails.

That idealization was refused by the new dramatists. Writing immediately after the scattering of the Armada, with the Queen at Tilbury still an incandescent memory, and with the Hakluyt reports, the newly-printed *Arcadia*, and the Red Cross Knight to enthuse and direct them to the invention of ideal figures, they chose to do something quite different. They made the stage the medium of English epic. Epic, as Sidney had desired; but not epic as Sidney had desired it. To Marlowe and Shakespeare history was a tale of crime. The dramatists, coming to the consideration of the heroic, told the truth about it; chose the real in place of the ideal. To tell the truth about a foolish world they both laboured with the records and uncaptived themselves from the records: they went to the chronicles for truth; but if the material they found there was insufficiently colourful to catch the vicious reality of men, they modified or re-patterned it.

The truth about heroism is the reverse of heroic in any hopeful understanding of the word. This is the conclusion an audience must draw from Marlowe's histories or Shakespeare's. The *Henry VI* trilogy is a protracted essay on the theme. For the purpose of its demonstration, the trilogy allows that the earlier age of the fifth Henry knew at least what the heroism of con-quest was: had fought and given and taken wounds for the public rather than personal advantage. Some sur-vivors remain to exemplify the code. In the course of *Henry VI*, Part I, we see them removed. Old Salisbury is shattered by a cannon-ball at Orleans.[7] Old Talbot and young Talbot, who might have continued his work, go under at Bordeaux, abandoned by the new generation of realists, men out for their own skins or their own aggrandisement. In the crucial fourth act, when the Talbots could be saved by reinforcements, York and Somerset in turn refuse to send rescue, because each hates the other and sets the private feud above the national need. The audience is reminded repeatedly of Sir John Fastolfe,[8] who skipped from the battle of Patay without delivering a blow.

The wolves are now loose. At the outset of the second part of *Henry VI* only one man cares for the nation: the young King's Protector, Humphrey of Gloucester. Not a man at Court supports him. The nobles, hating each other, combine to disgrace him, eject him from office, and murder him, so that they may have a clear field, the watchdog gone, to fight each other for the throne. Warwick, who, by his deliberate negligence, shares the guilt for Gloucester's end with the Suffolk faction, uses the Protector's murder as his *casus belli*, and as realists do in their heroycall furies, sanctifies his move with the name of Christ.[9] When the battles devastate England, there is heroism enough in the simple sense of sword- and axe-play, but in that more elevated and civilized sense for which the idealists and the Arthurian tradition seductively sue, there is nothing. At least there is noth- ing on the part of the heroes. A simple, rather naïve academic or cleric, young Rutland's tutor,[10] is perhaps the only ideal hero of the Civil Wars. He offers to die with his charge and has to be dragged away by troopers. Then the 'real' hero of the Lancastrians, Clifford, takes the boy's life. In due course the 'real' heroes of York hack apart the boy Prince of Wales and keep the balance even.

Heroes are butchers, nobles are ignoble. This is Shakespeare's picture of history on the threshold of the nineties, that period of national élan as the textbooks have it. It may be protested that he is picturing a dead century, and one which he and his contemporaries re- garded as the worst in the English experience, and is doing it as admonition in the best national interest, helping to preserve his own age from the destructive civil war incipient in its religious differences. Yes. In *Henry VI* and *King John*, as in *Romeo and Juliet*, the Elizabethan apprehension of a city divided against itself can be felt, and the appeal for unity is palpable. But while this may be the manifest purpose of the presenta- tion, the consequence is an enormous realization of a truth not localized in the fifteenth century: that the real world at all times is a world of self-interest and violence, and that ideal heroism is a delusive name. (Some years later Shakespeare dramatized an ideal heroism in Hector, the better to show its fate, its brutal beating down by the 'real' heroism of Achilles and the thugs.) Every poet's writing of history derives from his observation of his own world; and Shakespeare's record of what was is an account of what he has seen in Stratford or sees in Whitehall or on Cheapside. The dishonesty of the public men in *Henry VI* reflects his opinion of the public men of 1590. The demagogy which, throughout his life, he loves to expose is demagogy he hears mouthed. It is illustrated not only in the celebrated scenes of the Roman plays, but in the earlier plays we are now examining. Talking Jack Cade's Kentishmen into voluntary submission, the Duke of Buckingham and Clifford follow familiar gambits:[11] exploit the name of Henry V, long dead, to tap the past affection for the throne, and allege a foreign invasion to close the national ranks.

It is open to question whether the audiences who heard the players, and the readers who in rather later years bought and read the plays, shared the playwright's awareness that the evil past had its counterpart in their present. I believe they did. Dr. Forman's diary[12] shows that some theatre-goers, then as now, often came away with a fuzzy idea of what they had seen; but not all can have been fuzzed. First, the generations-old patronage of sermons accustomed them to the habit of applying the past to the present. Secondly, the fact that they watched the plays acted in the dress of their own day heightened their ability to see the drama in the terms of their own day. We may bear their skill in relating past and present, their willingness to think of all events as repeatable, in mind when we assess the pious close of *Richard III*. For the sake of courtesy and to pass the censor a Tudor playwright had to maintain that the disorders of England were rectified by the victory of Henry Richmond. But he did not mean it. He knew very well what had happened to Henry Richmond's sons: one, the hopefully-named Arthur, dead early, the other beset by marital disasters and a feeble heir. He also knew that within recent years Elizabeth had yielded, realistically, not idealistically, to political necessity and beheaded her kinswoman, Mary of Scotland. If family disasters pointed to a curse brought on by evil, the disasters of the sons of Henry Richmond declared their father's evil; and if evil entailed a curse, a curse must be gathering from the wrong done to Mary. No one in England could say this, but who could refrain from thinking it when they saw a Shakespearean history? And they thought rightly, as England's seventeenth-century history shows.

Between the writing of the *Henry VI* trilogy and the writing of *Richard III* Shakespeare developed the concept that crime caps crime, curse caps curse. He wasn't clear about it in *Henry VI*; he is clear in *Richard III*. The effort of working on the chronicles has stirred his mind and he sees an ancient pattern in English as in Old Testament and in Attic history. *Richard III* propounds the concept with a loud singing, a volleying to-and-fro of symmetrical lines, symmetrical couplets, that make some scenes more like opera than drama. This experiment complete, he rests from the handling of the theme (but not, perhaps, from his reflections on it). He decides to free himself from choric symmetry and excess of emphasis. Then with a finer, though this time an over-fine, instrument, he turns to *Richard II* and begins to write of the descent of the crime through the house of Edward III, as if in the wrong done by Richard to his kingdom and the wrong done by Bolingbroke to his King lay the first destructive exchange. Again he corrects his instrument: leaves the thin exactitude of *Richard II* behind and moves into the panoramic fullness, where all seems so loose, so openhandedly large and random, and is really so close-knit, and into the rich, analytical regional and psychological exploring, of *Henry IV*.

By now we are beyond the early 1590's and on the flood of the second half of the decade, when Shakespeare is the easy master of many characters, many voices, and has not yet begun to set himself the further problems that exceed the urgent needs of the time and tempt an artist who has satisfied the needs of his time. I would like to look at one work of this middle period: *Henry V*. My claim that the poets of the nineties are not simple idealists breaks down if the critics in general are right about this play. It is a familiar position that the Shakespeare of *Henry V* is the exponent of simple heroism and ardent chauvinism. 'The first great blast of the trumpet of English patriotism in literature', declares Professor Sisson.[13] To sustain which verdict he has to dismiss the opening act of the play as 'long paraphrases from Holinshed in which Shakespeare for once was mere journeyman'. As if the playwright who among all playwrights was most adept in bringing every scene to bear on a central objective would, after ten years in the profession, write an unbalanced history with a negligible first act. In every word of the first act there is, if we listen, a subtle urgency. Shakespeare tells us clearly that the King's war against France is unjust and unscrupulous. We recollect the second part of *Henry IV*, and know that Hal, no longer a delinquent Prince refusing to play heir to a father who committed treason and murder for the throne, has taken on his father's sceptre and his father's guile with it. He is acting without delay on the old fox's dying counsel: to concoct a war with France and so solidify the nation behind him. Even foxier than his father he plays Parliamentary politics with the Church: obliges the Church to take the apparent responsibility for launching him against France; and the Church assents, to protect its temporal wealth. This is the background of Hal's war: the usual background of wealth-cornering and power-piling, pursued under the banners of a blasphemed God and a falsified jurisprudence. If the jurisprudence is not false, the worse the King's situation. Shakespeare gives a good deal of care and time to a lucid rendering of the King's claim on France, which depends, it will be remembered, on his repudiation of the Salic Law. Shakespeare, who had twice already in other plays[14] told the story of Mortimer's claim against Bolingbroke, must have perfectly well seen that if the kings of England could demand France by descent through the female, Mortimer was entitled to England by the same right, and consequently that Hal was a usurper, while the Duke of Cambridge, whom Hal puts to death in Act II sc. ii, was the nearer heir. Evil on evil besets the play of *Henry V* as much as Shakespeare's other chronicles. A pure trumpet blast.

And yet the popular feeling about the heroism of the play is not all wrong, though some critics have puffed and inflated it in their touchline enthusiasm. Shakespeare concedes that there is such a thing as heroism, though it is not exactly trumpet-like. It is the quiet glow of cheerfulness in the face of danger, like old Sir Thomas Erpingham's,[15] or the dogged willingness of soldiers to do well despite their searching critique of the king's responsibility.[16] From the point of view of the recording angel it is the quality which makes man at his best in the face of the impossible or in defence of the lost cause. From the point of view of Shakespeare's audience it is a renewal of whatever in the experience of 1588 was by strenuousness made clean. It is almost a justification of God's way to man, of the violence in the universal structure. With that spurt of human fire at the core of the political mess comes a moment of cleaning. The parasites who followed the army 'to suck, to suck',[17] are run out of camp or strung up. Voices of decency are heard. But evil was paramount in the beginning and, though half-exorcized, will flow again. Having accepted his father's cult of intrigue, Hal has brought on himself and the nation a son who will lose all.

In fact, God interprets Hal's prayer, 'Not today, O Lord',[18] with a Greek care for detail. For that day God postpones the expiation he requires of the house of Lancaster and the people of England. Hal knows that nothing more than postponement can be asked. Only 'not today'. So much grace is earned by courage, humility, self-probing. But expiation must be made.

Does all this blot Shakespeare's patriotism? I hope it blots some of the more familiar accounts—but the patriotism it doesn't blot. The man who honours reality loves his country not the less for knowing the bad reality. Love is not love which alters when it alteration finds; and there is an obvious sense in which it is proved the greater by its patience with reality. We are not to play Coriolanus and quit Rome for detestation of its magistrates. Shakespeare, observing and dramatizing the evil agencies around him, is still a national poet. Gaunt's 'scepter'd isle' speech[19] is not fraudulent. Among the tasks of a dramatist—John Osborne takes it on sometimes—is to represent the passionate nostalgia of old men; and if he does it well he will understand, and make us understand, the element of truth in the poesis, the witness to a value in the life of the past; and he will make us feel that the very value which always seems to the speaker to have slipped away with his years, may still be alive under contemporary forms for the younger listeners. The images of Gaunt's speech, especially the allusion to Eden, that Lost Cause, are felicitous at two levels. Shakespeare writes Gaunt's speech with an objective fidelity to the habits of large minds in age and near death, and with a subjective entry into the values of England that Gaunt thinks lost in the welter of new evil and that his own Elizabethans, he too, feel present even in the welter of old-new irremediable evil.

Shakespeare untiringly holds, intently watches, the scales of good and evil. It is a work of Atlas. In the one pan the immense, accumulating slag of evil. In the other, apparently flimsy and nearly frivolous by comparison, an assortment of intuitions, decencies, graces, energies. Nothing, it might seem, solid and voluminous enough to counterpoise the evil. By the mystique of art the light, the little, and the occasional do sometimes outweigh the imposing, the terrible, and the unremitting. But he certainly does not set against his observation of evil any great structure, any one version of the good life, any coherent system of values. Elsewhere in this book I shall note how the critics of the last thirty years speak of Shakespeare's concept of order and the Chain-of-Being. They would call this his counterpoise; indeed they would say that evil is always subordinate to this. I will say at once here that I do not believe them. The Chain-of-Being is a chimera of our classrooms, which makes nonsense of some of his plays. The Chain-of-Being served Spenser beautifully. It supported an idealizing poet of the 1580's and early 1590's. It was no solution for a realist and empiric.

We can see Shakespeare exploring in different plays for embodiments of virtue to stabilize a troubled commonwealth. He tentatively works with one figure, then another, as his sources or the potentialities of his plot afford opportunity. One of his tentatives is a country squire, blend of the Horatian and English types, content with a small orchard, ready to use his ample muscle in its defence:

I seek not to wax great by others' waning,
Or gather wealth I care not with what envy:
Sufficeth, that I have maintains my state,
And sends the poor well pleased from my gate.[20]

Shakespeare does not repeat Alexander Iden; he is an idealization, and must go; but a later idealizing age, the

eighteenth-century, will copy him. A figure whom
Shakespeare does repeat is the quiet man of a modest
but exacting profession and a gnarled shrewdness to fit
it: the scrivener of *Richard III*,[21] the gardener of
Richard II.[22] These men cannot be hoodwinked by
demagogy; they see the truth. On the other hand,
though they can read their society, they cannot influence
it. The humble priest of honest counsel is a figure whom
the Shakespeare of the nineties appreciates, but who
disappears from the later Shakespeare, to be replaced
by a modern secular equivalent, the good doctor (conceived or strengthened in conversations with Susanna
Shakespeare's husband, Dr. Hall).

While the early Shakespeare can think of a friar as a
helpful figure, he never, early or late, proposes a religious faith as a stabilizing force. He writes, here and
there, a poignant line in evocation of Christ,[23] rather as
Marlowe, at a higher pitch,[24] has that poignant cry of
Christ's blood streaming through the firmament; but
no more than Marlowe does he expect the divided
Christian religion to check civic evils. The evidence of
life will not let him. It is not merely that the irreligious
at best disregard religion, and at worst exploit it, as
Warwick invoked Christ against Suffolk. It is that those
who care most deeply for their faiths do most violence.
His Europe was wracked by them: the fires burned alike
in Toledo and Geneva; and armies were tramping and
pillaging in the interests of zeal. No stabilization there.
But a power almost as abstract as religion, and often as
weak to check violence, seems to have had the hopeful
attention of Shakespeare for some years: the Law. If all
heroes were gentlemen, and if there were enough of

them, the world would have no need of law. In fact, we
have had to invent the law, which is never wholly successful but is better than anarchy. In *The Comedy of
Errors*, in *The Merchant of Venice*, and above all in
Henry IV, the law is a fixed point on which all depends.
It is the keystone of the civitas and of the play. The
king himself must acknowledge and preserve its supre-
macy. But after a decade of gravitation towards the ideal
Shakespeare withdrew or half-withdrew. Once more the
ideal was too difficult and too dangerous. Perhaps he
withdrew from it on the death of Elizabeth and the
arrival of a new hero (who was certainly no gentleman),
James Stuart, and the quick extinction, *pour encou-
rager les autres*, of the cutpurse on the King's south-
bound progress,[25] and the crash of Raleigh.[26]

A realist poet may undertake the hunt for stabilization but he will eventually abandon it. Wherever there
is virtue in Shakespeare's dramas, it is, as the common
phrase goes, 'its own reward'. Whether it belongs to
the variety that is fatal to its possessor, like the law-
abiding patience of Humphrey of Gloucester or the
powerless well-wishing of Henry VI (which becomes
less childish and more deeply-felt as the experience of
war strikes home), or whether it is the variety that can
defend itself, like the loyalty of Kent, its satisfaction lies
not in what it accomplishes but in that it *is*. By its loneliness it is a kind of heroism. What could be more realist? In the next century Milton's virtue is 'its own
reward': he fights his personal Agincourt in defence of
God, and is heroic not because he is right but because
he is on the losing side and because he is finally
alone.

I have been pursuing a distinction between the idealization of Spenser and the realism of Shakespeare and
Marlowe. Both methods of making tend to move the
world towards something a little better than the preval-
ent brutality. At the hinter-cerebral level both operate,
with entirely equal opportunity, by suggesting an image
or a 'shape' of intricate perfection; and they do this,
regardless of the overt meaning of their statements, regardless of the morality of their material, by the perfection of their craftsmanship; and the audience hungers
afterwards for a life consonant with the 'shape', and is
dissatisfied with a life that falls short. But both also operate at the cerebral level. Here the Tudor realist has an
advantage over the idealist. The idealist 'instructs'; but
with every hortatory gesture he is as likely to create
resistance as much as to evoke emulation. The realist
appears to destroy; but he destroys by a continuous
activity of the intellect, which excites an effort towards
an equal activity. Marlowe and Shakespeare look critically at their characters, and every action they require,
every sentence they invent, reflects their sceptical and
mobile thinking. Shakespeare's comedies are as analytical
as his chronicles and tragedies. That consummate early
work, *Love's Labour's Lost*, illustrates from start to finish
the alertness of mind that lets no phrase or dogma pass un-
scrutinized. In Marlowe's *Dr. Faustus* the vital curiosity
turns on itself: the play is a critique of the over-daemonic intellect by the over-daemonic intellect. So much the
better. The Tudor stage is self-critical as well as critical.

I do not want to over-value the cerebration. Matthias
Shaaber not long ago combated the academicizing of
Shakespeare by stressing that the plays function *viscer-*

ally.[27] That is right. We should pursue good performances, at the English Stratford or the Ontario Stratford, in London or in Bucharest (which a friend tells me has the best national theatre in Europe), and live them viscerally. They strike at the viscera through every movement and grouping of the actors, every gesture and answering gesture; and through the rhythms, intonations, and tunes of the words, in fact through the Apollonian song of which the early 1590's proclaimed the mastery. But they do aim at the intellect too, aim at it and involve it, all the better for the visceral reactions, which liberate and galvanize it.

The mind of Donne was sharpened by the plays he saw as a law-student playgoer in the early nineties. Dr. Faustus, Dromio and Dromio, Petruchio, Mercutio and the grasping kings, made him *him*. There is no question that the dramatists quickened any genius who came to hear their work. Of course a genius was quickened. But was the ordinary public? Were butcher, baker, and candlestick-maker quickened and changed? Shakespeare might be quoted against the likelihood. He describes the collective demos as the enemy of intellect. Jack Cade's clubs hang the Clerk of Chatham for writing[28] and Lord Say for patronizing education,[29] and the Roman mob dismembers Cinna the poet.[30] But he was reflecting there on the extraordinary obliteration of the individual light when the mob runs; was anticipating the modern studies of the crowd. I suppose that individuals, and even groups—small groups: the family, friends in twos and threes, tables of diners, benches of drinkers—must have been quickened and enlarged by the nervousness and the thoughts that followed a play.

43

I submit, though you may regard it as mere idealization, that the realists, by example, not by precept, helped to endow the England of the next four centuries with its peculiar mind: notoriously unsystematic; but sceptical, shrewd, flexible, capable of improvisation, capable of soaring. But again I add that the work was done not only by the intellect of 1590 but by its song.

The Merchant's Dark,
Hamlet's Winter

IT was a habit of Shakespeare's to do more and other than the occasion of a play required. A modest case is that of *A Midsummer Night's Dream*. The requirement was specific: a play to entertain a wedding-party. Shakespeare concocted a work of sympathetic magic to fertilize the wedding; and over and above the essential of the piece, the stimulation of his audience by the dance of error through the Anglo-Cretan labyrinth of the dark forest, he added a model of the child to be conceived when bride and groom got to bed. That is, he drew Theseus as a model, the energetic Theseus, amoral in love but in public life the noble protector of common folk (an ideal Theseus, for in comedy Shakespeare sometimes allowed what he would not easily allow in history). And then, following his instinct through the glimmering wood to a point never before visited by a writer, he found the symbol of the rustic's love for the queen, the idiot's love for civilization, the mortal's love for the immortal—a symbol which Chagall in this century assimilated to his own lifelong image of the fool and the White Bride.

A more striking case is that of *The Merchant of Venice*.

The comedy of *The Merchant* arose from a melancholy occasion. In 1594 the Queen's chief physician, Roderigo Lopez, who was descended from a Spanish

Jewish family, had been accused by Essex of participation in a Spanish plot against her life, had admitted receiving money but had denied any intention of harming Her Majesty, had been found guilty and sentenced to death; and, after some weeks of delay in which Elizabeth seems to have considered mercy, the efforts of Essex had prevailed, and in June the sentence had been carried out after the ferociously spectacular manner of the time. The Rose Theatre had capitalized on the events by reviving Marlowe's *Jew of Malta*. Apparently Shakespeare's company thought it necessary to offer a competing attraction. Shakespeare was asked to provide a script.[1]

Shakespeare gauged the requirements of the occasion as some rude satisfaction for the rougher public, some scarcely less rude and vigorous satisfaction for the Essex adherents. He was, after all, himself a satellite, however remote, of the Essex party and lived in hope of advantage from the connection. It was his obvious strategy to caricature Lopez as an enemy of the people. He looked round for a story on which he could impose a grotesque and dangerous Lopez. He found a story which Ser Giovanni told in the fourteenth century,[2] of a gentleman who at third seeking won a wealthy lady despite her wiles, forgot in married bliss the godfather who had signed a perilous bond to finance his expedition, remembered at the latest moment and hastened home, whereupon his lady, following secretly, turned lawyer, and all ensued much as we have it in the play. The critics have not decided whether he read Ser Giovanni in the Italian of the 1558 printing, or whether he used an English version, perhaps already cast in dramatic form. If he worked from the original or from a version that followed the original treatment, he made a radical twist of his material. Ser Giovanni kept Giannetto (his Bassanio) and the lady (his Portia) in the foreground of his tale from start to finish; his merchant was a godfather indistinct but for his gentleness, his Jewish moneylender was indistinct but for his hostility to Christians. Reserving the young man and the lady for his subordinate plot, Shakespeare brought the remoter figures to the fore and, while yet uncertain whether he could deepen their characters, saw his way to the enlargement of the moneylender's outline with the emphatic stage-strokes that exploit the crudest mediaeval prejudices against Jewry: Shylock fearing for his hoard and repeating 'Fast bind, fast bind'; whetting his knife at the trial; resenting Launcelot Iobbe's[3] appetite (a comic touch but one which shows that Shakespeare had never known the hospitality of a Jewish table).

The story he had selected obliged him to transfer the events from the political plane of the Lopez intrigue to the economic. What he lost in topicality by the switch he gained in opportunities for vulgar agitation. The financially-expansive, financially-adventurous London of the nineties was a London crushed by interest.[4] After an often-recurring pattern he planned to blame the alien in the community for the financial mess. His Lopez-Shylock would be the economic enemy. The next step was to oppose him with an equally popular, equally incredible economic hero. Ser Giovanni's gentle millionaire, sitting in a counting-house among partners and factors, changed into Antonio, a business-man who is exempt from the business-mind: who seeks no thrift; who lends without interest; who makes a mission of redeeming debtors from lenders. Antonio would be the knight on a white horse to the rescue of London. He would be a light that never was on sea or land.

The two impossible figures Shakespeare had imagined were sure to win the favour of the crowd. Neither could please his analytical mind. He turned to the supporting plot, and here his attention moved more freely, for it offered people who might be treated with the shadings, sometimes delicate, sometimes pathetic, sometimes nobly firm, that he had already developed in his comedies. Above all, it provided a heroine. She already possessed, in Ser Giovanni's tale, vitality and generosity, a teasing good humour and love. Once adopted, she ensured that by the virtue of the light she threw on the cruder characters, the play would go at least some distance beyond the popular melodrama the company and the hour seemed to want. Of 'wondrous virtue',[5] she diffuses suggestions that mildly rebuke the fever of commerce and the raving of crowds: moralizing imagery of the gifts of the leaden casket and the lovely gifts of girls (your ships should sail in quest of them, not the golden fleece).

The two plots are linked by Bassanio, who, as the original tale sets it out, can only woo the lady at the peril of a merchant who loves him. Let the merchant be not a godfather but a passionate friend to Bassanio, and the way is prepared for a sentimental question dear to the Tudors: the debate of 'god-like amity'.[6] Choosing between his friend and his girl, ought not a lover to give his greater loyalty to the former? Shakespeare had tried his hand at the topic in *Two Gentlemen of Verona*, where he had implied by the line of his plot that an honourable man (but there will only be one honourable man in any two) will prefer his friend to his girl; but by his characterization he had implied that women have such courage, intelligence, and fidelity that they must be preferred to any man. A riddling solution: but it secretes a truth, that the lover will do injustice to someone whatever he chooses. The topic 'Man-friend or girl-friend?' is a Tudor pattern for illustrating the impossibility of complete virtue in an imperfect universe. Like the ode of Simonides which Socrates discusses in the *Protagoras* it says that it is hard to be good. Twentieth-century authors are concerned with the difficulty of knowing the truth; knowing the truth has replaced being good as literature's statement of the human purpose. But whatever the purpose, literature always answers that it can't be done: you can't be wholly good; you can't know the whole truth. Shakespeare knew that he had handled the theme piquantly in *Two Gentlemen*. It was contrary to his professional pride to do again what he had already done well; but perhaps he was dissatisfied with the abrupt ending (if indeed the last scene of *Two Gentlemen* is his; it may be a botched abridgement) and was glad of a chance to display a neater treatment. Or he may simply have grasped, as he grasped at his heroine, at matter which he could handle with pleasure and with his skilful mixture of gaiety and wisdom, and felt infinite relief at the diversion from his melodramatic merchant and banker figures, which seemed intolerable to him despite their box-office material. (It will be understood that I am speaking of a dynamic process; attempting to break into the creative act at a relatively early point, at which Shakespeare is still considering what he will write and making and remaking the plan.) The outcome of his pleasure is that he leads Bassanio, who is more naturalistic than Ser Giovanni's fairy-tale hero, towards goodness—not far towards, but as far as life can permit or a little further. Forced to the choice between old, absent friend and new, present, desirable and desired wife, Bassanio rises above his native carelessness and makes the severer choice. He chooses the friend. And Portia approves. A woman cannot let her husband off scot-free if he has the hardihood to prefer god-like amity, and Portia and Nerissa make their husbands smart a little for the impudence of virtue; but all the same they know that the men are doing the best that men can do, and respect them.

The sub-plot activated Shakespeare's imagination. His glands flowed more freely. By letting his fancy withdraw from the horror of current events and play the games of comedy, he became capable of looking more carefully at Antonio and Shylock; and now he sensed how to humanize and deepen them, not least by bringing to bear his own distress at his own greed by which he made art and money out of intrigue, prejudice, and death.

At the start of *A Midsummer Night's Dream* Theseus banished melancholy from the festivities. At the start of *The Merchant* Antonio declares it for his mood, confesses himself a wearisome 'want-wit'. One function of this beginning is to spring the exposition of the ships at sea, the situation that leaves the merchant unable to help his friend unless he resorts to Shylock. But the discussion of melancholy and the moods of men goes on for another hundred lines after Salarino and Salanio have described the ships and their perils, and apparently Shakespeare is doing several things concurrently in his customary way. Q and Dover Wilson in their Cambridge edition of 1926[7] explain Antonio's melancholy in terms of the debate of amity: Antonio is downcast because he has learned that Bassanio is in love; is jealous, afraid that he may lose his friend. All the more beautiful his underwriting of the embarkation for Belmont: a conquest of self by which amity is veritably god-like. The explanation is excellent and has helped the modern appreciation of the play. But it touches only one component of the melancholy complex. Antonio is melancholy because Shakespeare has perceived, by the process sketched in the last paragraph, his own melancholy. But this is a misleading way to put it; for it might seem to say that Shakespeare, suffering with those who suffer the oppressions of the world, pours his feelings into Antonio and makes him a great sympathizer. This is exactly what he does not do. His Antonio is still, what he was planned to be, the representative of those who sought Lopez' conviction and applauded his death. In anger at the proceedings and at his own complicity in them, Shakespeare wants to deepen and darken Antonio and yet he must preserve his popular status as Shylock's heroic opponent. He contrives this double feat.

The extensive opening discussion in the first scene ranks Antonio among the extreme characters—they are to be called, three or four years later, after another dramatist has brought his genius to bear on them, 'humour' characters—who are a danger to themselves and to society. In a quick Theophrastian essay written for Salarino, Shakespeare points out the extreme dispositions with which some men are endowed at birth:

> Now, by two-headed Janus,
> Nature hath framed strange fellows in her time:
> Some that will evermore peep through their eyes
> And laugh like parrots at a bag-piper,
> And others of such vinegar aspect
> That they'll not show their teeth in way of smile,
> Though Nestor swear the jest be laughable.[8]

And to prove this point Gratiano arrives immediately: Gratiano, the loud laugher, who stands at the opposite end of the scale from the austere Antonio. In annotation of Salarino's oath, 'by two-headed Janus', Dr. Warburton wrote about 'those antique bifrontine heads, which generally represent a young and smiling face, together with an old and wrinkled one, being of Pan and Bacchus; of Saturn and Apollo, &c.' Not an extraordinary note; but Dr. Johnson thought it worth repeating; and it calls attention to the opposition of temperaments which straddles the play; and is suggestive to actors, to directors, and to the critic. A Shakespearean comedy often questions the extremist. Beatrice in *Much Ado* says that an acceptable man would have a little of Don John's melancholy and a little of Benedick's prattling.[9] She doesn't mean it in good sadness, she is scoring off Benedick rather than painting a hero; but the play proves her words more significant than she intends: Benedick learns to leaven his wit with purpose. A rather similar movement takes place in *The Merchant*. The immediate advantage to Shakespeare of the distinc-

tion made in this first scene is that it establishes a
system which counters his main (and hated) system of
scrupulous Antonio battling unscrupulous Shylock.
There are four extremists in the play: Antonio, Shylock, Gratiano, Jessica. Antonio and Shylock, equally
and similarly at fault, represent one wing of extremism:
they are melancholy, vinegar, saturnine. Gratiano, loud,
quipping, allegro, leads the other wing. And with him is
Jessica. Jessica's rôle is an oddity of the play; perhaps
it begins merely as an imitation of Marlowe's Abigail;
and it proves, like Launcelot Iobbe's coarse humour,
how little Shakespeare knew about the Jewish world.
But Shakespeare does know a great deal about father-
daughter relationships in general; and he makes dramatic sense of Jessica by showing how a daughter whose
father has compelled her to watch his treasure, and has
watched her because she is part of his treasure, reacts
against the vigilance and parsimony and breaks out.
Jessica's flagrant prodigality, once she is free, is an act
of recoil from her father and the prison of his fast-bind-
ing proverbs. Between the extremes stands the golden
mean, Portia of the golden curls. She has her moments
of imperfection, which all the better prove her human;
but she is a nice blend of thought and energy, serious-
ness and joke. And Bassanio? He begins the play with
the prodigals, is a spendthrift and dowry-hunter; but he
has some notion of measure, as his early rebuke to
Gratiano suggests, and he grows to genuine friend and
truth-telling husband. By his example the play promises
—since a comedy may make promises—that men can be
educated from their excesses towards the middle way.

To preserve Antonio's heroic status Shakespeare

writes a splendid aspect into his extreme melancholy. His melancholy is austerity. It is cognate with Shakespeare's image of Rome. Antonio has the upright stance, the unshakeable integrity of the Romans. Bassanio decribes him, with love and admiration, as

> one in whom
> The ancient Roman spirit more appears
> Than any that draws breath in Italy . . .[10]

The actor should sustain throughout the performance a demeanour that warrants these lines. It will stand out at its best during the trial. Some of his faction, notably Gratiano, behave disgracefully during the trial, but Antonio is 'arm'd and well-prepared'[11] with the Roman fortitude. His melancholy becomes his nobility. And in so far as a play about a merchant is a commentary on the new merchant society of his era, Shakespeare offers a ghost of a claim that the men of the emergent class are, if less than noble by blood, noble by character: by plain living and high thinking, by a spirit of inextinguishable strength. This is almost a salute to Puritanism by a Shakespeare who, belonging to a profession that fears the dour theological Left, makes very few such salutes.

But if the melancholy is splendid, it is also destructive. Shakespeare effects a transposition of the dismay he feels at the world into the violence that leads to the deeds that evoke the dismay. Antonio's dour severity is too proud. It modulates too rapidly into intolerance and violence. He is not content with his refusal of the code of thrift. He feels bound to hate it, and to hate its practitioners with a religious hatred and race-hatred. He spits and spurns. 'You call'd me dog',[12] Shylock reminds him, asking in effect why favours should be exchanged except between friends, and gets the fierce answer

> I am as like to call thee so again,
> To spit on thee again, to spurn thee too.

This may be heard as the melodramatic box-office Shakespeare currying the applause of the Londoners with a demagogic flourish, or as the discerning Shakespeare following the psychological activity of his simple hero who turned out to be complicated. What begins as a man's virtue, his robust refusal to acquiesce in the general wealth-grubbing around him, may become his vice when pride turns it from quiet self-containment to a crusade against the other man. The melancholy is the fatal flaw which moves the play. It accounts for the feud between Antonio and Shylock; and, exhibited in its rudeness in the bargaining scene, it results in the bond. Antonio in his contemptuous probity actually demands a bond by which he may be damaged:

> If thou wilt lend this money, lend it not
> As to thy friends; for when did friendship take
> A breed for barren metal of his friend?
> But lend it rather to thine enemy,
> Who, if he break, thou mayst with better face
> Exact the penalty.[13]

This is a long step from Ser Giovanni's simple story, where the bond and its enforcement against a good-natured godfather are entirely the doing of the usurer. And even at the trial the demeanour that is beautifully heroic is still contemptuously heroic. The would-be panegyric of the heroes of the Essex camp who root out the enemies of the public has become a tragedy, and the popular Quixote designed to rejoice the crowd has become an ungentle tragic hero. Shakespeare conducts this comedy in his tragic manner—alike for Antonio, by pursuing the ambivalence of his dominant quality, and for Shylock, by heaping up his motives (just as he heaps up motives for Hamlet or Iago). Shylock's crime is to insist on an inhuman vengeance when a whole city beseeches him for mercy and offers double and triple compensation. But the cause is manifold: a lifetime of suffering, years of interference by Antonio, the insults that Antonio throws at him with the bond; and in case we still think this insufficient, Shakespeare adds the seduction of Jessica, her theft of his wealth, the news of her prodigality after his years of thrift, the symbolic tossing away of Leah's turquoise. With so much to hurt him Shylock must hit back at the Gentiles, and is grateful that he has their champion and icon in his grip.

Some good critics have maintained that the point of the play is that 'must hit back' is an inadmissible expression:[14] that the new Christian dispensation teaches mercy and not revenge. This would be well if the play's hero were sufficiently Christian. Antonio has one claim to represent the Christian sweetness: it is his love for Bassanio, his readiness to break his custom for his friend and to risk his life for his friend. But his severe melancholy, and the sheer violence to Shylock which is consistently its outcome, accord with stoicism or with Puritanism but not with the New Testament. Shakespeare saw that excessive virtue was fatal to Antonio's position as a Christian hero.

On the impulse of the perception he worked through the play one of those general propositions that are the intelligence of his comedies. He sets it in circulation through Portia. No sooner is she on stage than she is making the point:

> It is a good divine that follows his own instructions. I can easier teach twenty what were good to be done, than be one of the twenty to follow mine own teaching.[15]

Religious standards in their higher versions, whether Christian or Jewish or Moslem, are never practised. Shakespeare does not know enough about the Jewish world to know where Shylock falls short of Jewish morality. But he knows his Christian world, its standards and shortfalls, and he does the self-critical work that the standards of art require. Antonio's contempt, Gratiano's roaring, are Christian self-criticism. In the trial-scene, with its rhythm of argument and counter-argument, triumph and counter-triumph, he gives Shylock a clear point against the hypocrisy of Christians who, evangelists of brotherhood, maintain, oppress and market slaves:

> You have among you many a purchased slave,
> Which, like your asses and your dogs and mules,
> You use in abject and in slavish parts,
> Because you bought them: shall I say to you,
> Let them be free, marry them to your heirs?
> Why sweat they under burthens? let their beds
> Be made as soft as yours and let their palates
> Be season'd with such viands? You will answer
> 'The slaves are ours:' so do I answer you.[16]

In the famous passage in which Shakespeare feels completely with Shylock and asks from within Shylock's character 'If you prick us do we not bleed',[17] the argument amalgamates a sense of common humanity and the act of Christian self-criticism: 'If a Jew wrong a Christian, what is his humility? Revenge. If a Christian wrong a Jew, what should his sufferance be by Christian example? Why, revenge. The villainy you teach me, I will execute'. And he adds—for Shakespeare remembers Portia's formulation of the theme—'and it shall go hard but I will better the instruction'. The play becomes a critique of the norm of preaching virtue and perpetuating crime.[18]

What takes over in the daily neglect of the higher religions is an ancient code of self-seeking and self-protection. To know something of the Shylock of whom he knew nothing, Shakespeare had thought over, perhaps re-read, the book of Genesis, describing the earliest condition of the human race, the origins of Israel, the struggles of Jacob, the ethics of the sands before God dictated the Law to Moses on Mount Sinai. The name of Shylock may come from Genesis xlix, 10,[19] the names of Tubal and Chus come from Genesis x, 2 and 6, the name of Jessica may come from Genesis xi, 29. More important, there came from the reconsideration or re-reading of Genesis the friction of a disclosure to Shakespeare about himself and about society—the provenance of the names is only meaningful as attesting the provenance of the thought. It quivers furiously in the speech which is the epicentre of the bargaining scene. This is Shylock's first scene. Our impression of his character and outlook must be formed by what he says. He tells the story of Laban and Jacob:

> mark what Jacob did.
> When Laban and himself were compromised
> That all the eanlings which were streakt and pied

Should fall as Jacob's hire, the ewes, being rank,
In end of autumn turned to the rams,
And when the work of generation was
Between these woolly breeders in the act,
The skilful shepherd pill'd me certain wands
And in the doing of the deed of kind
He stuck them up before the fulsome ewes,
Who then conceaving, did in eaning time
Fall party-colour'd lambs, and those were Jacob's.
This was a way to thrive, and he was blest:
And thrift is blessing if men steal it not.[20]

It is one of those Old Testament stories such as appalled
George Moore when he came to read them in middle
age, and appalled Bertrand Russell when he found time
to read them in prison, stories which do appal until we
see their vital lesson. The lesson of 'kind', that is, of
nature, may be translated 'Men must do whatever must
be done to live' or 'The first duty of man is to survive
and propagate'. If as Tillyard once said, Shakespeare
writes his best poetry when he is seized by a character
or an argument, he is seized at this point. The passage
is superb and has no equivalent elsewhere in his early
and early-middle work; the bizarre idiom is a poet's
response to the Bible, the Biblical feeling only modified
because the writer is an Englishman who has never seen
the desert, but who lets the experience of a boyhood
among the Warwickshire farms operate in substitute.
For Antonio he has written the traditional charge
against usury: that it is wrong because unnatural:
money does not breed. Shakespeare might have elaborated on the tag, educed its meaning. But he did not.
For he had discovered in his reflections on Genesis that
he himself was a sort of Jacob. He was a breaker-away

from obedience, a wilful survivor, a wilful prosperer, a tiger's heart wrapped in a player's hide. Sometimes a merchant of sorts, he more closely resembled Shylock than Antonio. He gave his attention, and awoke ours, to Shylock's answer.

It seemed to him to explain the way of the world. To the law of 'kind' or nature we revert, regardless of the later and higher laws we have been taught or teach. We aim at 'thrift' under the drive of 'kind'. Your cuckoo sings by kind, your merchant trades and profits by kind, your politician pushes to the top, stays there, and enforces his advantage by kind. Usury is no worse than any other deed of kind; it is obedience to the thrust of nature; whereas kindness in the sense of charity is a defiance of nature. Keenest practitioner of the quibble in an age that loved 'a tricksy word',[21] Shakespeare could not resist the pun on kind and kindness, which ricochets about the bargaining-scene. Kind and kindness represent the two ideologies of the play.

But though Shylock's answer explained Shakespeare to himself, and he was then able to go on to the marvellous near-entries into Shylock's suffering and tenacity of will, he does not quite justify Shylock, precisely because he cannot quite justify himself. He becomes a divided mind. He feels the heroism of the wilful survivor, as the power of the speech shows, and he knows that the force within himself is heroic in the same degree. The action of the tiger is magnificent. To that extent he aggrandizes the thrust of kind. But he deplores the failures of men. Those critics who have spoken of the contrast between the Old Law and the New are wrong if they claim that the New Law is

exemplified by the play, but they are right if they say
that the New Law is desiderated. It is the unmistakable
tragic lament of the play that we have heard of the New
Law and pay lip-service to it but never practise it.

The melancholy that stains the play from Shakespeare's tussle with the occasion and the exigencies of
his parasitical craft becomes the night that invests the
play. The darkness of *The Merchant of Venice* is the
antithesis of the aphrodisiac darkness of *A Midsummer
Night's Dream*. That early fantasy of the dark forest and
the fairy webs glittering at the change of the moon, a
chrysalis hour of death and rebirth, which Shakespeare had spun to exhilarate and exalt bride and bride-
groom, to get them god-getting in an enchanted sympathy with orient and occident, past and present, he has
now reworked as a moral fantasy. The play is a para-
digm of a bad world—or, as Portia says, a naughty
world:²² a world in which we do to one another what
Antonio did to Shylock, what Shylock did to Antonio,
what Essex did to Lopez.

There are glitterings in *The Merchant's* dark. The
masquers flame through the streets. The moonlight fills
the terrace; fades again. The stars inlay the heaven.
After the trial, with its harrowingly naturalistic display
of the ferocity of kind, Shakespeare offers a scene of
lyrical and reflective exchanges. Every newcomer to the
play is captivated by the moonlight on the gardens and
the Ovidian antiphonal in which Lorenzo and Jessica
out-night each other; then there follows a self-repre-
hending time when we doubt whether we should like
this passage: is it adornment? is it fake adornment in a
play so nearly a lynchers' play? But it is right. It warns

61

of the presence of the harshnesses of kind, such as we
have just witnessed at the trial, behind the lyric indul-
gence and the talk and fondling of love; tells of their
presence throughout history. The lovers whom these
lovers invoke are unhappy, players with sad parts on the
world's stage. The argonaut who turns his prow towards Colchos and the golden fleece may bring home
Medea. Still, this is a comedy. Bassanio has reached,
and subsequently deserves by his efforts at honest faith,
not a Medea but the lady of Belmont, the candle-flame
of whose hall is the 'good deed in a naughty world'. The
'good deed' stands against the 'deed of kind' which
generates cut-throat life. In the last minutes of the
comedy, however, Shakespeare throws this opposition
to the winds: there is a burst of lovers' bawdy, and
Portia and Nerissa will take their husbands to bed to
the game of the ring and the deed of kind. It is as if,
having half-promised man's amendment by the grace of
comedy, he forgets or changes his mind and chooses the
lustihood of comedy and says that nature must have the
last word.

An artist has often to be satisfied with the beauty of
his arrangement of the terms of a problem. It has to
serve him instead of a solution. Marvellous how, out of
bad circumstances, out of attempts to get away from
them into familiar comic systems, out of much recasting
of his intentions, out of unreconciled judgments that lie
crisscross over each other, Shakespeare made a play at
once powerful and elegant. But soon after the first performance and his pleasure at his feat, he must have been
irritated by what he had not done. By the discovery of
the conflict between civilization and kind he had risen

above the needs of his occasion, but he had not examined the conflict as closely as he would have wished, and his popular comic ending had simply laughed it away in excitements of the blood. He would have to try again.

He carried into *Hamlet* the work originated in *The Merchant of Venice*.

All that Shakespeare's company required of him for *Hamlet* was a revenge play. The standard notion, which he had once pursued in *Titus Andronicus*, would have done: the notion that a great man, having suffered terribly at the hands of his enemies, feels bound to make them suffer equally in return; it seems to him, as it seemed to the primal peoples of the Mediterranean scrub or the saga-peoples on the fells of the north, that Astraea will not come back to earth till crime has been answered with crime; and though it is difficult, so powerful and guarded are his opponents, he overcomes the obstacles with tenacity and cunning, and balances the scales of justice by revenging himself with the exact due of ferocity. In *Hamlet* Shakespeare repeats the pattern of the terrible provocation ('a father kill'd, a mother stain'd'); sets the play in Denmark where pagan practice and myth out-stalk Christianity; shows that every brave young man, like Fortinbras, of whom we hear at once, and Laertes, whom we watch in action later, avenges his father's murder. But then, having created the conditions in which revenge appears necessary and 'natural', he makes his hero hesitate: hesitate not at outer difficulties, for he takes care to show that Hamlet has access to the King, but at inner; and not by weakness, for he takes care to prove Hamlet's courage and strength, but by virtue, though a virtue which Hamlet himself does not understand. This peculiar refinement of the revenge plot arises, I suppose, from the coalescence of memories of *The Merchant*. Certainly the traces of the memories are observable. The great problem of *The Merchant* had crystallised during reflection on Genesis. Here again Shakespeare thinks of the events and tone of Genesis, and especially of the story of Cain 'that did the first murder'. In *The Merchant* he had made 'thrift' and 'kind' his keywords. In the first act of *Hamlet* he uses them again, with the bitter punning of *The Merchant*. His gloom at the occasion of *The Merchant* had led to a suffusion of darkness. He pulls a deeper darkness around *Hamlet*: Hamlet's sable; darkness of the battlements; darkness of the corridors abutting on the hall where 'The Mousetrap' is sprung (the King shouts 'Give me some light' to escape down the black maze); midnight of the King's chapel and the Queen's closet; the leafless and raging night of the Scandinavian winter. At the moment when he approached the task of a revenge-play, he must have remembered that Shylock was a revenger, have remembered writing the lines in which Shylock justified his case against Antonio by the Christian addiction for revenge. He had thought extensively on *The Merchant's* problem in the intervening years. He now brought the thinking to bear.

Attempting to get deeper into the problem, Shakespeare involves his tragedy in tangles. In *The Merchant* the men who think they are Christian and civilized are controlled by archaic thrusts of which they are scarcely conscious. This corresponds with our normal contrast between the rules of civilization ringing at the top of the head, known to us but not honoured, and the primal thrusts buried in the psyche and the stronger and more dangerous for operating out of sight. But in *Hamlet* the drive to revenge is the rule in the head; the impulses to civilization work as unconscious forces. This is bound up with a central difficulty: that revenge is really a middle term between 'kind' and civilization. For desert-man or saga-man revenge is a step towards civilization, a rough justice, which corrects the thrust of a murderer or a raping Tarquin. For a Christian or Tolstoyan, a Buddhist or a Quaker, and in some hours for Shakespeare groping through his intuitions, it is itself an act of kind: it allows a man to kill the killer, which is to live his appetite; and, since retaliation follows retaliation, it leads to an endless chain of crimes (the chain of crimes which Shakespeare dramatizes and deplores in the chronicle-plays). Hamlet, a saga-prince, consciously regards revenge as the rule. It is justice; of course it is nature too, but it is common justice. He nowhere criticizes it. Yet he defers the killing of Claudius. What a man does is what his deeper self intends. His delays must mean that he would rather not kill the King. For this reason Kenneth Muir can write that Hamlet wanders on 'the blank page between the Old and New Testaments'.[23] And by this reasoning Hamlet's tragedy is that he eventually kills the King. And this is true, if a part-truth. An unconscious but beautiful resistance to killing holds out for a time, then is over-run. Professor Muir's epigram, however, would make Hamlet's subterranean quest for civilization entirely Christian, whereas Christianity is only one component of his dream.

There is some drift of Christian feeling in the play.

It is at its strongest in the first act. The winter that wraps the battlements when Horatio and Marcellus join the sentries may be the season 'Wherein our Saviour's birth is celebrated'. The glow of the morning—in that metaphor of the 'russet mantle',[24] which critics sometimes regard as the dramatist's lapse into a youthful stylism, but which is thematic—may be the promise of a new light, a better dispensation. But it is in fact, as any shepherd could tell Horatio, the sign of a coming storm. On these same battlements the Prince follows the ghost and hears the beginning of his story. At once the saga-man is stronger than the Christian and swears to sweep to his revenge. Christian feeling continues to exert a pull, but a weak pull from the depths, perceived but not understood. When Hamlet calls on the forces of the universe for witness and strength, he falls into struggle with himself:

> O all you host of heaven! O earth! what else?
> And shall I couple hell? O fie! hold, hold, my
>   heart;
> And you, my sinews, grow not instant old
> But bear me stiffly up . . .[25]

The expletive of repugnance, the nausea, and the effort to brace up against the nausea, are signs that the Christian is resisting the saga-man. A simpler saga-man, Laertes, eventually makes the situation clear:

> To hell, allegiance! vows, to the blackest devil!
> Conscience and grace, to the profoundest pit!
> I dare damnation.[26]

Laertes has worn his religion lightly and sheds it easily. The restraints of Christianity are more intimately grown into Hamlet. But he feels them obscurely, construes them in an inverted, negative form:

> Who calls me villain? breaks my pate across?
> Plucks off my beard, and blows it in my face?
> Tweaks me by the nose? gives me the lie i' the
>   throat,
> As deep as to the lungs? who does me this?
> Ha!
> 'Swounds, I should take it.[27]

Every insult of the enemy might be answered by turning the other cheek, as the oath, by Christ's wounds, begs us to remember. Hamlet does not recognize his own argument. He travesties the virtue as it talks to him and through him, and it slips away. The divine birth, heralded in the imagery of the first scene, proves a dead birth. Shakespeare has not much greater confidence in the transforming power of the Christian impulses than when he wrote *The Merchant*. Yet he has spoken what can be spoken for them more emotionally, more earnestly. They have not been utterly null. They have exerted a check on the Prince for the duration of half the play.

They restrain Hamlet with the help of another and stronger force, one which found no place in the drama of *The Merchant*: the civilizing intellect. Hamlet is far more an intellectual than a religious prince. He is a university prince. The title-page of the first quarto of 1603 claims that the play was acted not only in London but in 'the two Universities of Cambridge and Oxford, and elsewhere'. It is rich in university material and a perfect university play. Deprived of the university, whether by his father's bankruptcy or by his own indifference to formal education, Shakespeare makes a point in *Hamlet* of showing off his skill in disputation; he wants to manifest himself a born reasoner who could have been the best student of them all. The university manner, which he mimicked from brother-dramatists, friends, perhaps relatives, and from talk heard and sights seen when he lay over at Oxford en route between Stratford and London, glances vivaciously through the script. But Shakespeare is not merely emulating the manner. He is speculating; he is asking what the cultivation of reason, the pursuit of knowledge, can do. Religion, instead of purifying corrupt man, had itself fallen to the world's corruption. But at Wittenberg, Hamlet's university, Faustian man in the shape of Luther had found enough audacity and strength, not to change the world but at least to reform religion, to shake and divide old institutions and inaugurate new institutions from the fragments. Whether this meant that Faustian man could alter primal man was not so certain. But the Wittenberg name, the university reasoning, the touches of university friendship and fellowship, moving through the first half of the play and lending Hamlet sparks of energy and charm to offset his depression and to commend him to an audience, mean that Shakespeare is considering whether an answer to the question debated in *The Merchant* is to be found here.

The play praises reason. Where 'amity' was 'godlike' in *The Merchant*, reason is 'god-like' in *Hamlet*.[28] Without it 'we are pictures, or mere beasts'.[29] You cannot speak of reason to the Dane and lose your head. But praise of reason is easy, its practice and application are as difficult as the practice of religion, and wherever the

word occurs in the play it occurs in a baffling muddle.
Hamlet sees it upside-down, as he saw the doctrine of
turning the other cheek. He appeals to reason because it
is the star by which he set his course in the better days
before the storms of the funeral and his mother's re-
marriage, but he appeals to it when he is in a passion.
His outburst when he has viewed the transit of the
Norwegian army is typical: he speaks as if 'reason' led
Fortinbras to the invasion of Poland, and as if 'reason'
were his own spur to the murder of the King. He em-
ploys 'reason' as if it meant an almost angelic faculty,
whereas it now means no more than the ability to discern causes:

> how stand I then
> That have a father kill'd, a mother stain'd,
> Excitements of my reason and my blood,
> And let all sleep . . .[30]

It means 'I have due motive for revenge—by the saga-
code'. With the skill of the classrooms he juggles with
the future-looking 'reason' to make it mean less than it
might and to endorse the rough justice, the conventional
crimes, of the past.

He both mobilizes the classroom skills to the enforcement of revenge and blames himself for pursuing
the classroom habits of question, scrutiny, and analysis,
and testing the case for revenge. He calls his 'thinking
too precisely on the event' three parts cowardice. But
thought has served him well, restraining him from a
crime unacceptable to a civilized man, of whom the
scholar is, in this context, an emblem. How ingeniously
thinking has sanctioned his delays and compensated
them by affording the activist in him (and thereby

affording the drama) heaps of substitute action! It has worked with the Christian impulses, and performed the greater share of the work, in checking the Prince.

To check the Prince 'for the duration of half the play' is obviously a limited accomplishment. Still, something is registered to the credit of the civilizing virtues; they put up a contest against man's natural violences. But the moment we set the middle of the play against its end, we encounter a terrible implication. If indeed what a man does is what his deeper self intends, then while it is true that a Hamlet who glimpsed a better practice than revenge intended his delays, it must also be true that the Hamlet who in the final tally killed not one victim but seven, and himself to make an eighth, intended the carnage. And it must be true that the deepest Hamlet of the carnage exploited a semi-deep Hamlet, the Hamlet of the delays, for the ultimate, result. The death of Claudius was not a sufficient prize for the angry Prince. He wanted more. The antics which ingenuity provided as surrogates for murder seemed good delaying tactics to the scholar Hamlet of the middle depths. The violent Hamlet allowed them because they must alarm the guilty Claudius into counter-measures and so gradually create the situation for the general massacre. Mines below mines!

Shakespeare anatomises the deeper violence clearly, especially by the juxtaposition of two scenes,[31] one displaying Hamlet still under the check of his scruples, the other displaying the conditions under which the check ceases and he strikes his first blow. When Claudius is caught alone at prayer, and 'Now might I do it pat' and Hamlet's sword comes out, the intellect deftly allies itself with the residual Christianity and persuades Hamlet to delay: 'Up sword and know thou a more horrid hent'. Then Hamlet comes, at the witching time of bed and begetting, to his mother in her privacy. Inflamed by the rage of two months spent brooding on her submission to his uncle, he lays hold of her with excitement. Then the male voice, the male shape, behind the curtain. Night-battle of toms; the thrust of kind. Death of the rival male by a blow which denotes the taking of the woman. It is a consummation; and it is the pivot of the play. The chain of counter-stroke and counter-stroke is forged from this first killing. Claudius, at this demonstration of violence, of which he feels, with the certainty of guilt, that he will be the next victim, must retaliate. The saga-son, Laertes, must retaliate. Their initiatives will provoke Hamlet to the ferocities so long deferred, and yet, foreseen from the start (his first speech to us is a speech against his mother), so precisely, by oblique tunnellings, attained.

The secret of *Hamlet* is that the conflict which appears to be fought out, between kind and civilization as represented by crude revenge and the impulses to a higher life, is a mock-battle. In the utter deeps kind is in command. It is driving Hamlet to kill his mother. Even the saga-code of revenge is civilized by comparison with that drive, which the father-ghost, representative of the rude saga-principle, forbids. But kind is strong beyond all opposition, will conscript every other principle to its own fulfilment. This is a grim verdict to which Shakespeare comes as he thrusts with perplexity, constantly reinforcing his intuition with recollections of the corrupted currents of the real world around him, through the tangles of the problem. A fiercer verdict than *The Merchant's*. To *The Merchant's* lesson that religion is weak and goes under, Shakespeare adds that the intellect, for all its agility, is the destitute cat's-paw of kind.

The portrait of Claudius confirms the sentence on the intellect. Claudius is a capable King. His control of the Norwegian crisis is masterly: a rapid arming of the Danes, a diplomatic démarche with well-briefed ambassadors. As a man he is by no means slight, though Hamlet, with a partisan fury, says so. Somewhat like the mediaeval Ganelon, he has stature, might be a hero were he not a 'traitor' and were he not undermined by his guilt. (If he had not reacted against Hamlet's sallies and probes, and if he had forbidden Polonius to interfere, the chain of events by which Hamlet zigzagged to the killings would never have begun; but guilt compelled his reaction.) Ambition for the crown and lust for the Queen unseated his judgment. Throughout the play he exhibits, the more clearly for the occasional successes of his reason and statecraft, the melancholy of reason shattered and ashamed of its fall. The visible symbol is his drinking, of which Hamlet speaks with contempt and which a director must show on the stage. The auditory symbol (since Shakespeare had a liking for 'noises off') is the cannonading at every bumper of Rhenish downed. Memory and reason are drowned in the wine, thinking disconnected by the sudden salvos. The prince who asked leave to go back to Wittenberg and the progressions of the intellect is detained where thought must be broken.

A felicity of the play, if we measure by what is plaus-

ible, and a horror, if we measure by what is desirable, is
that Hamlet eventually welcomes the interruptions and
the subjugation of the intellect. There is a side of him
that wants to be the uncomplicated saga-son, natural
successor to his warrior father. He loves the physical
life, the sword, wrestling. The university has suggested
other means, other ends. But since the higher life suspends the vigorous ancestral life, he is glad of everything that suspends the claims of the higher life. Intellect can be tripped and stifled by a sudden attack, which
elicits the instinctive riposte and the fight for survival.
A probe by Rosencrantz and Guildenstern, a treacherous letter, Laertes' imprecation and leap into the grave:
surprised by these Hamlet does what he would not do
were he given space to reflect. Olivier grasped this
essential when he filmed the play; his treatment of the
Folio's rough stage-direction, 'in scuffling, they change
rapiers', depends on it. Laertes, who has been unable to
hit a pleasantly sportive and nimble Hamlet, suddenly
thrusts at him after the umpires have called a pause.
Hamlet gazes at his bleeding arm, senses the treachery,
and, typically converted by the provocation from his
civilized to his saga self, attacks furiously at the next
play; disarms Laertes, takes the poisoned foil, makes
Laertes accept his clean foil in exchange; then both
fight for their lives till Hamlet strikes home. It is, for
better and worse, not true that Hamlet 'takes it' when
someone plucks his beard or tweaks him by the nose.
He is grateful, exactly because it frees him to give up
the confusing and paralyzing road to civilization, frees
him to strike back and strike home.

As the play grimly evolves Shakespeare decides not

only that the nascent intellect will be blotted out but that it will of its own consent re-establish the barbarians in its place. The university intellect is a democracy of the mind. 'Friends, scholars, and soldiers', the Prince called Horatio and Marcellus, and he greeted Rosencrantz and Guildenstern 'My excellent good friends . . . Good lads . . .' He was right to withdraw his affection from Rosencrantz and Guildenstern when, in their angling with 'ambition', he saw that they were spies.[32] But was he right to send them to their death? Right to tell the story to Horatio without a jot of commiseration? There must be a touch of doubt and commiseration in the voice of the purer Horatio when he turns the thought over: 'So Rosencrantz and Guildenstern go to't',[33] but there is none in the strenuous, jeering reply 'Why man, they did make love to this employment'. He who stood for fraternal health has become the destroyer. He is free now of civilization, its refinements, and restraints. From the events on shipboard, the sense of danger that kept him awake, the raid on the despatches, successful by the fineness of his muscles, not his brain, he has learned to drop his attachment to reason and prefer the rashness he once despised in Polonius. 'Praised be rashness', he sums up, 'Indiscretion sometimes serves us well'. By its winter contest, its winter journey, the mind has come to condemn the mind. Hamlet's sentence of death on the intellect is confirmed in the fold-up of the play. The last decisions, the last farewells, forget that he was ever 'scholar'. He orders Horatio to live and tell his story, believing that the world will think him justified—think that he has 'reason' in the low sense of 'motive'—in the deaths that he has pulled around his ears. Diminishing the goodness of the forgiveness he and Laertes have exchanged, he throws off a crackle of ebullience: 'I cannot live to hear the news from England':—as if the assurance, 'Rosencrantz and Guildenstern are dead', would make a dying man laugh. An energy of mischief has usurped his scruples. And finally he emits, and this is determinative, the energy of statecraft: a political act in the tradition of the old King Hamlet or Claudius. He names Fortinbras to to the throne of Denmark. Fortinbras is not a man of the mind. He belongs to the procession of the Scandinavian warriors. No university for him, but lawless resolution, quarrels of honour, the doctrine of the sword. Hamlet's last decision is to let the old hard world go on in the old rough way. Better its brutal vigour than the quiddities and quillets of the chambers or the lecture-room.

'The Humanists hoped', says G. K. Hunter in his book on Lyly,[34] 'that a man could be made fit for responsibility in the great world of experience (that is, prudent, just, wise etc.) simply by a course of scholastic discipline'. By this test *Hamlet* is an anti-Humanist play. If at a theatrical level it is the tragedy of *Hamlet* that Hamlet ultimately kills the King, at the ethical level the tragedy is that Hamlet decides, with a university ingenuity, against the university dream of a world civilized by intellect.

Only: Shakespeare's grim verdict is not the total sum of his play. Why do audiences and readers respond to Hamlet in all his thinking and talking and suffering and eruptions of vigour, and participate, with imagination aspiring at full stretch, in his last exchanges with Horatio, and hope that flights of angels sing him to his rest? By virtue of his beauty. But in what does his beauty consist? Sometimes in his energy: there *is* beauty in the action of the tiger. But it cannot lie solely, or mainly, there, for fighting vigour is a gift he shares with Fortinbras and Laertes, and his light outshines theirs. His beauty must be sought in what distinguishes him from them; and this is his scrupling intellect. Though it has not been strong enough to subdue the powers of nature, nor to track these and descry their ambush, and though he has condemned its perplexities and at last abandoned it, it has been his genius. The personality glows against the darkness in which the play ends. A failure, but beautiful in his winter landscape, he has pointed to some greater beauty for which we hope, some alliance of the abundant physical life with the wisdom to do nothing when action would add crime to crime.

Eliot was of course wrong[35] when he wrote that *Hamlet* was an inadequate vehicle for the difficulties Shakespeare fought out in it; eventually he must have known that he was wrong, and presumably he kept the essay alive for the theory of the objective correlative, not for the theory's erroneous application. *Hamlet*, in its tangles, intricacies, inversions, in its levels of meaning mined by levels of meaning, was the perfect equivalent of Shakespeare's perturbation at the helplessness of what is gentle before the onrush of what is rank and at the treacheries that are inseparable from the virtues they invade, the perfect equivalent of the troubled shifting of his opinions as now he defended himself for his fight with the angel, his merchant passions, his rash enterprise, now hated his iniquity, now justified the spiritual mêlée by the music to which it led: struggling with himself he burrowed through deeps below deeps, as Hamlet does. And yet when Shakespeare contemplated the work in retrospect, he still could not be satisfied. He had written with much greater complexity than in *The Merchant* and had fought his way to a harsher conclusion; but again to a split conclusion. Where it was harsh, was it harsh enough? Where it was split, could it be true?

He lay restless under his dissatisfaction, and turned back to the same problem in *King Lear* and explored the relationship of nature and society for a third time; and again ensued a collision and fractures, of which I shall say a brief word in the last chapter of this book.

A major comedy and two major tragedies resulted over the course of ten years from the thinking set moving in Shakespeare by the events of 1594. May it console Lopez in the shades to know that these works are his creation and his memorial! But to say so is to follow the escape-route which Shakespeare took into beauty, the artist's consolation. It was a favourite Elizabethan route. Whether art can ever make up for the pains of life, for the reality of an Elizabethan career, for the exertions that lead to rewards, but then to a trial and an execution, each man must decide for himself. In Shakespeare's England there were some men who valued the 'grace' of a perpetual name above 'the disgrace of death'.[36]

1599: The Event and the Art

AT the beginning of June, 1599,[1] the archbishop of
Canterbury and the Bishop of London consigned certain satires and other works of literature to the flames,
banned any further publications of the kind, and im-
posed a censorship on histories. A well-known book by
O. J. Campbell, *Shakespeare's Satire*,[2] depends on the
point that the Bishops' Edict can hardly have gone un-
noticed by the leading dramatist of the day. But Dr.
Campbell's reconstruction of Shakespeare's response to
what was after all a crisis for playwrights and poets, a
crisis that affected them all regardless of their rivalries
and factions, strikes me as not quite in accord with the
spirit of the plays he discusses. From every good critic
we take something with gratitude and leave the rest,
and with Dr. Campbell's help we recognize that the
event of the spring of 1599 must have left a mark on
Shakespeare's work, and proceed to our own guesses.

A scene in *As You Like It*, the seventh of the second
act, defends the functions of 'taxation', that is, of satire.
Jacques is the speaker. His arguments are in essence
two: that satire is society's medicine, to 'Cleanse the
foul body of the infected world'; and that it is no libel,
for the crime is its target, not the guilty individual, who
is pained and reformed in the privacy of his soul and
suffers no public damage—unless he loudly protests or
calls for withdrawal of the charges, in which circumstances it is not the satirist who exposes him but he who
exposes himself. Speculation on the question of Shake-

78

speare's reaction to the Bishops' Edict may reasonably start here.

Jacques' speeches sound like Shakespeare commenting against the repressive Edict on behalf of his fellow-craftsmen. Nor need Shakespeare be the less sincere if, as Dr. Campbell says, the defence coincides with that employed at the time by the dismayed satirists. On occasion Shakespeare was evidently willing to serve as spokesman in a professional matter. The passage in *Hamlet*, in which he argues for the adult actors against the aery of children, is a familiar example.[3] With this more famous case the 'taxation' dialogue of *As You Like It* bears comparison, except that in *As You Like It* Shakespeare is the advocate not of one section of the writing guild against another, but of the whole guild against the censorship. In both plays the action is suspended to allow the presentation of the arguments. Both presentations are astute. In *Hamlet* the arguments are vivid and concise and claim to be in the 'best interests', as spokesmen always allege, of the children themselves —since the child actor will eventually be an adult actor. In *As You Like It* the arguments work not solely by their force, though they have some force, but by their very incompleteness and the imperfections of the speaker. This perhaps sounds peculiar, but a glance at the text will clarify it.

Jacques offers to cleanse the world of its blemishes. The Duke thrusts in an argument against him: 'You yourself were a libertine, and now you want to be a moralist: you want to indulge both ways!" Some editors take that interruption very seriously. Dr. Sargent, the Pelican editor, finds that the Duke 'rises in anger'. But is it not, simply and pleasantly, that the Duke is 'disputable'? He enjoys his follower's tirades and is ready to prompt them: 'I love to cope him in these sullen fits'. When he accuses Jacques of 'mischievous foul sin in chiding sin', it is not anger. It is calculated ribbing, for the amusement of the discussion and for the intellectual vistas that the exchange may open. In fact, the Duke's conduct is precisely the right conduct for the mature ruler: to encourage his taxing poet and listen to him. It is a model to the Bishops, who might do the same by the nation's satirists. 'Do as this good Duke does', Shakespeare's scene implies.

Jacques finds no answer to the Duke's sally. He dodges it and persists on his former tack. By letting Jacques miss a trick at this moment, Shakespeare shows his own experience in debate, not to say in demagogy. He knows that his English audience will incline to the man with the rickety equipment. The English love the losing side. Melancholy Jacques is more after their heart than sack-drinking Falstaff. Jacques has the typical long face of rainy England. Typically he has gone into exile with his king, as the English, often conquered, often driven to Sherwood Forest, believe a good man should: the obligation is recognized throughout Shakespeare's drama; in *Antony and Cleopatra* it is avowed in a speech that reverberates with the tradition, directly descended from Anglo-Saxon poetry:

> he that can endure
> To follow with allegiance a fallen lord
> Does conquer him that did his master conquer
> And earns a place i' the story.[4]

Jacques is a funny 'old gentleman',[5] but that does not

make him, what Dr. Campbell imagined, a figure of contempt. Alike for his fidelity, his temperament, and his imperfection, Jacques has the audience with him. He is eccentric, for he is a poet, and he would not be a poet, would not be a permanent satirist, if there were not some maladaptation. He misses the secret of the golden mean,[6] as Rosalind tells him, and he forgets to criticize himself, as Orlando tells him.[7] Sometimes he is too dour; a gayer, sounder satire can be heard in the speeches of other characters, Celia often, Rosalind often. All this is not to damn him, but to ensure that the audience approve the defence of satire the more because the satirist is imperfect, and accordingly acceptable.

The 'taxation' scene may, of course, have been an addition to an existing play, revised for the stage in 1599; we cannot use it to maintain that the whole play was written that year. Yet it is not isolated. Rosalind has already, early in Act I, tried to curb Touchstone with the threat 'you'll be whipped for taxation one of these days',[8] and Touchstone has hit back 'The more pity, that fools may not speak wisely what wise men do foolishly'. This too might have been interpolated in a 1599 refurbishing. But my impression is, that the question of satire is not superimposed on *As You Like It*, but informs the organization of the play. In the following paragraphs I shall imagine, leaning on the scholars who, for various reasons, have dated it between 1598 and 1600, that *As You Like It* was composed under the impact of the Edict; and while I shall remember that another wing of scholarship assigns it to an earlier year, just after Marlowe's death, I shall suggest that the

Marlowe allusions fit 1599 and are connected with Shakespeare's attention to the smoking satires.

But why would a dramatist concerned to say a word for the liberties of his profession broadcast his appeal from the woods of Arden? Possibly, because there could be no better camouflage. Shakespeare was a loyal trade-unionist, prepared to query the new regulations on behalf of his fellows; but he was also a canny individual, who often advised himself to keep in the rear of his affection, and, if he made a protest, insured against its hazards. When the actors voted that something be done about the event of June 1, he asked himself what kind of play would most easily slip by the authorities in their current state of vigilance. The solution: pastoral. The Elizabethan nineties were the heyday of English pas-toralizing: three editions of Sidney's *Arcadia* had appeared; minor poets, such as John Dickenson[9] and William Smith,[10] had been 'transported into the blessed soile of heauenly ARCADIA' and into 'passionate Eclogue'; *Aminta* was still ravishing English wits, and its successor, *Il Pastor Fido*, had lifted the ravishment to a new level. There was security in modishness. A pastoral idyll would be the least suspect to the censors.

For double insurance Shakespeare took his plot from *Rosalynde*,[11] dedicated by Lodge to 'his most esteemed Lord the Lord of Hunsdon'. Light romantic meanderings, which Hunsdon, Lord Chamberlain and, in theory, Shakespeare's master, had accepted nine years earlier—self-evidently no one could find mischief there!

The pastoral convention adopted, Shakespeare scrutinized it. He scrutinized it with that mind not given to mere repetition of other men's conceptions, rather to their dissection and to re-synthesis in new surprising terms. He now wrote his own variation on pastoral. He took up the pretence that the country is better than the town; sketched it, in the Duke's greenwood life,.with a temperate joy; and then questioned it in a series of passes between his courtlings and the country-folk! Questioned it, called it in doubt with a few striking illustrations, but declined to destroy it. Shakespeare knew both country and town. He had been brought up on the edge of Arden, where

> We equally partake with woodland as with plaine,
> Alike with hill and dale; and every day maintaine
> The sundry kinds of beasts upon our copious wast's,
> That men for profit breed, as well as those of chase.[12]

He had darted off to the metropolis, and had spent nearly a dozen years there, tasting the advantages and the dolours. He was later to give up the town, choosing to retire and die where he began. In 1599 he makes it clear that for the man who has seen both ways of life, the choice, if a choice must be made, is not hard: the country is less evil. He endorses the Renaissance experience—Skelton's experience, and Wyatt's—that the life of the Court is corrupt. The first act of *As You Like It* moves in Court and great house, and the perils of the urban milieu are made evident. Lest his audience has forgotten them after ninety minutes passed largely in the forest, Shakespeare works a reminder into the tail of the play: when Rosalind goes out to reassume her skirt and let down her hair, he has a gap to fill, and in his customary manner he turns his time-filling dialogue into theme-supporting dialogue: he writes Touchstone's cadenza about the Court and its poltroons. Against the

life of the Court a man would be an ass not to choose a
'low content'. It is a commonplace of the age:

Art thou poor, yet hast thou golden slumbers!
O sweet content![13]

On the other hand, as he brings his woodland groups
forward, Shakespeare dis-idealizes them. To this extent
he satirizes the pastoral convention. The rural life, as he
remembered from childhood, is a life of labour, not of
leisure or poetry; it is not timeless,[14] but time runs
heavy in it, even for lovers, who bring their serpent
with them wherever they go; it is not Eden, for it is no
perpetual spring, but suffers the pelt of rough weather.

Probably he expects us to go with him a little further
in the balancing of commonplaces. All men, whether in
London or Warwickshire, incur the chronic penalty of
seasonal change, effort and disease. Everywhere there
are fools: in Court a fop; in the sheepfold William and
Audrey. Everywhere there are persons endowed with
innate gentility, whose good manners reveal a heart un-
corrupted: Rosalind and Celia at Court; Orlando, deprived of schooling, but nevertheless mature in natural
manners and inherited dignity; Corin, the shepherd, a
model of courtesy and sense. Where Fortune's gift, the
social lot, is weak, Nature's gift, which is disposition,
may compensate.[15] Anywhere there may appear a
strength stronger than the environment. But virtue is
harder in the town, easier in the woods, which will do
something to heal the town's corruption, as the usurper
Duke is healed and converted when he crosses their
perimeter.[16] Shakespeare deftly modifies the pastoral
myth, bringing it a little closer to reality.

Closer to reality without loss of sweetness! Although

the great sentimentalists like Q have always said so, there *is* a sweetness in the play, which remains undispersed even if we view Shakespeare's wit as practical and sophisticated, and rather unsuitable for the junior school, where, in England at least, the Q mind often recommended the comedy for the syllabus. Q's reactions, and those of the headmistresses, are an acknowledgement of the success of Shakespeare's methods. Shakespeare has filled *As You Like It* with sweetness, intending that the sweetness be taken for purity. As part of his prudent 'insurance' method, he probably wanted to throw a dazzle around his criticism of the Bishops' Edict—a dazzle that would seem pure as a nimbus to authority, yet innocent of piety to his audience, to whom it would be no purer than sunshine. The requirement did not exclude some bright bawdy and the Ganymede crack, for sexuality was not of itself any impediment to purity (add a Thersites and the situation would be altered, but the Thersites element is barred). The play gradually unfolds as a hymn to the goddess of all goddesses pure: Juno. Early in the action occurs the phrase 'Juno's swans'.[17] The normal phrase, as the editors hasten to annotate, is 'Venus' swans'. Not by ignorance, certainly, nor by oversight, though he was addicted to oversight, but by policy Shakespeare has side-stepped Venus. The poet of *Venus and Adonis* has become the poet of Juno, guardian of wedlock. In her name Hymen appears and unites four couples.[18] What could more amply guarantee the propriety of the writers' guild?

This brings us to the Marlowe allusions. Among the elegies of Ovid, which Marlowe translated, there is one,

No. XIII of Book III of the *Amores*, which is a hymn to
Juno and her 'chaste feasts'. It contemplates the same
scene that Keats was to find on the Grecian urn, and its
excitement is clean. The *Elegies* of Marlowe were burnt
in the Bishops' offering on June 1, 1599.[19] Perhaps
they went to't only because they were bound up with
Sir John Davies' *Epigrams*; but whatever the reason,
their own merits or the dangerous company they kept,
they perished. I suppose that their demise affronted
Shakespeare; that he said, with the outrage of the intelligent man in every age when he tries to account for
occasional higher rulings, 'What could be found in the
Amores to trouble the realm!'; and that, fingering
through a copy of the volume, all the more to be prized
now that it was contraband, he came on Elegy XIII and
said 'A poem for Juno and chastity—and they burned
it!' The incident set the Juno scheme of *As You Like It*
shaping in his head. And it mobilized his memories of
the passionate shepherd and the great reckoning in a
little room, and led to the Marlowe tributes and the
assimilation, elegantly and touchingly managed, of the
line from *Hero and Leander*.[20]

The critics who judge that an allusion to Marlowe's
death could only be made soon after the stabbing, and
that the 'great reckoning in a little room'[21] puts the date
of *As You Like It* soon after May 30, 1593, have not
sufficiently allowed for the variety of operations of a
poet's mind. Besides a poet's immediate response to
an event, there are, *inter alia*, a gradual response,[22] a
revived response, and an amended response. I fancy
that the Marlowe allusions belong to one of the last two
kinds, and were elicited by the bonfire of June 1.

Of course, to introduce references to that scapegrace, Marlowe, was in some measure to unpin the safeguards Shakespeare was raising by writing a rural and prudential comedy. But here lies another quirk of a poet's mind. There are times when poets, and all artists, concede to their opponents and resist them, simultaneously and in the same work. Shakespeare does so here. He both walks warily and takes risks.

But he probably felt secure as he spun that sweetness that simulates purity. It is a sweetness distilled from good temper. Yet if I suggest that Shakespeare composed *As You Like It* in an effusion of good temper, I shall seem to stumble into a contradiction. I have been writing about a Shakespeare busy with the censorship crisis, and even annoyed by it. How, then, do good spirits come into the record?

They break and belly out from a hint in Lodge. Lodge's lovers and shepherds lived in the forest of Arden. Shakespeare, beginning the reconstruction of *Rosalynde*, realized that he could set his play in an English Arden: his native countryside. In every Arcadian fantasy there is likely to be an element of 'le vert paradis des amours enfantines'. The name in Lodge sent Shakespeare's thoughts homewards and two or three decades backwards, so that they moved among deep-impressed recollections of tree, field, and cottage, which proved exceedingly agreeable. Even his fall with Ann Hathaway acquired—malgré Joyce's marvellous interpretation of its dislocatory jolt[23]—a nostalgic coloration, and expressed itself as a 'foolish song',[24] which means a song the wiser for being light and gay. But Ann Hathaway was a relatively late experience. The

very early ones counted more. Arden was Shakespeare's
mother's name. Elsewhere in the plays there are mothers
so strong that one shies a little at the image of Mary
Arden; but evidently she transmitted positive influ-
ences, 'that feelingly persuade me what I am', and
helped her son to find himself. The forest of Arden is
not only 'l'innocent paradis' of the Warwickshire cop-
pices, but mother's lap. The whole congeries of childhood experiences deploys before Shakespeare as a
drama pleasurable and benign, and the asperity that
London and its affairs might have injected into the play
is mollified. A totally unforeseen gift of recourse to the
pastoral form!

The rush of good temper in the act of memory brings
another gift. It helps Shakespeare to an extended essay
in music. I must perhaps be careful not to exaggerate
here. Shakespeare tended at all times to musicalize his
dramas; and their music (in several different but related
senses, for, besides song itself, the tone of the writing is
involved, and the method of arranging soliloquies,
dialogue, and ensembles) is one of the qualities which
distinguishes them from other plays of their period and
from later plays. He had already gone far with the
process of musicalization in *A Midsummer Night's
Dream*. *As You Like It* is his furthest step. There are
several scenes which, were the dramatist's main consideration to carry the plot forward or to deepen our
knowledge of the characters, would be redundant. The
scene in which the huntsman is dressed in the slain
deer's antlers and the horn-song sung, and the scene in
which the two pages give their duet,[25] these do nothing
but augment the 'musicalization', supply the play with

tendrils of music and pageantry. *Rosalynde,* so stimulating to the dramatist in other respects, must again have provided him with the cue. Like Sidney's *Arcadia* and Sannazaro's pattern-*Arcadia,* Lodge's *Rosalynde* combined prose and lyric, the poems threading the prose narrative. Shakespeare recognized the charm of the combination, and resolved, by one of those acts of insight which came to him as he manipulated his sources, to experiment in a dramatic structure that emulated it. The good temper of which we have spoken, the good temper flowing from the Arden associations, made the work easy, and the lightly operatic result helped to communicate his mellow mood to the audience.

The same formal development had a thematic consequence. Speaking for his colleagues in protest against the suppression of their trifles, Shakespeare must have been set thinking about the real questions the whole fracas entailed. What subjects were right for literature? What were the boundaries of literature's business? Should a dramatist find ways of entertaining his audience which had as little as possible bearing on living issues? Or should he be 'a *material* fool',[26] that is, an entertainer whose words smote on live issues? It is possible to think of *As You Like It* as an experiment in material folly, the folly represented not so much by the clowning as by the music, which speaks to the sensations and not to the brain, and yet, while it has no means of discussing ideas or causes, adjudicates ideas and causes. There may have been a point in the early conception when Shakespeare thought of the music of his play as the cocoon which swaddled some young thoughts and carried them safely through a hostile climate. In the end, however, there was no such distinction between the music and the matter. The music of *As You Like It* is 'material' in at least two respects: while the words of the play debate the pastoral convention, the music defends Arcadia more effectively than words can; and the music continually directs the audience to the fundamental experiences of life, which are, unlike the battles of factions, inevitable, and which are simpler, keener, and purer, alike in their pleasure and pain, than the battles of factions, and which must always be kept in central view if any right decisions are to be made by the individual torn between the pulls of a complex urban civilization. The upshot of his experiment was the demonstration of one answer to his question about the right way of work for a dramatist in 1599: an admirable way of work, his play showed, was this blend of music and matter.

He could not know how, three hundred years away, his experiment would be debased; how the twentieth-century 'musical' would descend from *As You Like It*; how at its best it would dance such Arcadias as *Oklahoma*, offering Broadway the freshness of the golden world but not a mote of the intellectual adventure which made Eden habitable for Shakespeare; and at its worst it would be drained of all marrow, musical and intellectual.

As You Like It was perfect for the needs of June 1599. For Shakespeare not only gave reasons why poets should satirize and their masters and victims should listen, but wrote an ingenious illustration of a new, subtler satire. At the outset of these notes I differed from the scholars whose Shakespeare hoots at the epigrammatists. I cannot see him as the blackleg. What we might say is that, if he proved to the authorities that there could be such a thing as *gentle satire*, he proved it to his fellows, too, and that nothing could have been better than the practical example to urge them to some purification of their grosser art. Yet let us not overstate the case. His Thersites, whether drawn earlier or later than this date, outdoes them in grossness—all to the good. Even within the limits of *As You Like It* let us not overstate the case, and let us not reduce gentle to genteel drama, nor refine its satire out of existence. George Puttenham said of pastoral that the poets devised it

> not of purpose to counterfait or represent the rusticall manner of loues and communication, but vnder the vaile of homely persons and in rude speeches to insinuate and glaunce at greater matters, and such as perchance had not bene safe to haue beene disclosed in any other sort.[27]

We might almost construe Puttenham as saying that pastoral is always satire. He would have recognized a good example of the genre in *As You Like It*. The fact that the comedy is not only critical but self-critical—an essay in the criticism of the genre—makes it curious but the richer and none the less *echt*. It is in contact with *The Shepheardes Calender* before it and *Lycidas* after; it helps us to estimate both the merits and the weaknesses of these works; helps us to recognize that their insinuations and privy nips are part of the tradition and the poetry; helps us both to respect and shudder at their anti-ecclesiastical poetry, measuring its ferocity against Shakespeare's swift-thinking yet patient, diplomatic yet charitable, critical yet gay style.

The title of the play? Perhaps, a view which has Professor Bullough's concurrence,[28] it is related to a phrase in Lodge's preface to the reader. But it may be a sign of Shakespeare's pleasure in Tasso's *Aminta* and Guarini's *Pastor Fido*.[29] The first chorus of *Aminta*, 'O bella età de l'oro', had fascinated the Elizabethan poets in the late eighties and the nineties. Abraham Fraunce had translated it into hexameters, by no means negligible.[30] Daniel translated it into thirteen-line stanzas, brilliantly rhymed.[31] Shakespeare may be thinking of that chorus rather than of his favourite Ovid when he talks about fleeting the time carelessly 'as they did in the golden world'.[32] Guarini's counter-chorus, in which he matches idea for idea, rhyme for rhyme, was soon equally famous in England. Just how soon is open to investigation. Dr. Perella has pointed out[33] that Guarini was the cynosure of the Court-wits by 1605; was translated by 1601; was printed in London in Italian as early as 1591. Poets and their pleasure in virtuosity being what we know them to be, I will guess that during the nineties the Mermaid Tavern sometimes buzzed with comparisons of the two choruses, and particularly of the two climaxes at the twenty-sixth line. Tasso's twenty-sixth line announces 'S'ei piace, ei lice'. Abraham Fraunce translates it: 'If you will, you may'. Daniel: 'That's lawful, which doth please'. I, to bring out my point, 'If you like it, *licet*', or 'If you like it, why not?'. Guarini, whose chorus contra-affirms that not nature but law must be our guide, retorts 'Piaccia, se lice' – 'You like it when it's legal'. Shakespeare's play, with its commentary on the pastoral myth, is a contribution to the Tasso-Guarini debate. On which side? In so far as his characters fleet the time carelessly, on Tasso's side. In so far as his rural girls are coy and virtuous, not on Tasso's side. In so far as his play celebrates Juno and the rites, on Guarini's. But the title, *As You Like It*, is a tease: it gestures towards the Tasso and Guarini choruses and leaves us uncertain which climax he's citing. Deliberately. If the Bishops asked him, he replied 'Guarini, of course'. If you or I or Durrell asked him, he replied 'Tasso'.

"Twelfth Night"
with a Touch of Jonson

COMPARED with *The Merchant of Venice*, the most serious of the sentimental comedies, and even compared with *As You Like It*, *Twelfth Night* is apt to look a little empty. It does not address itself to the charged social problems, by success or failure with which civilizations grow or are snuffed out. But with a hand as light as that exercised in *A Midsummer Night's Dream* it sketches not an argument but a series of variations on the quality and fate of love. It is a forerunner of the modern novels that anatomize love, though it works entirely in the objective mode, they in the subjective. It is the completion of the myth of error that Shakespeare has been exploring for a dozen years: behind the physical errors that ensue when girls disguise as boys, and when twins go in identical fashion, colour, ornaments, it implies our blunderings in the pursuit of a quasi-Platonic perfection; and it excuses our blunderings. And it looks back to *Two Gentlemen* and resumes the theme, well and sweetly embodied in Julia, more roughly though not unhandsomely embodied in Valentine, of the sacrifices of love.

The Duke, Viola, Olivia, Antonio—these four characters love and sacrifice. The Duke, constantly renewing his protestations to Olivia, sacrifices rank, dignity, complacency. In the academic classrooms in recent time the Duke has been mis-read: condemned as an affected masochist, in love, as we brilliantly say, with love. To Shakespeare his posture is no more ridiculous than any other lover's . It is part of the humility of love to consent to absurdity. True, if we compare his love with Viola's it will seem less dedicated, but this fault is not private to him, it lies in his sex, as, being far less blinkered than his critics contend, he is the first to see and say,

> For, boy, however we do praise ourselves,
> Our fancies are more giddy and unfirm,
> More longing, wavering, sooner lost and worn,
> Than women's are.[1]

Shakespeare makes this point with his usual preference for women over his best men. Nonetheless, the Duke is worthy to be loved, is commended by Olivia although she cannot love him, evokes Viola's love at once. He is not in love with love, in any sense in which that condition would need remedy. To be in love with Olivia, who is sworn to grief for a brother lately dead, is to love the living semblance of melancholy; and Shakespeare draws him as if this love for sad beauty is a just commitment of the complete nobleman.

Viola's employment with the Duke is daily sacrifice. At the end when he discovers that she is not Cesario, he recalls the service done him so much against the mettle of her sex.[2] The phrase is kin to the service 'improper for a slave',[3] that Kent did for Lear. In *Lear* Shakespeare intends to show that Kent has devotedly nursed and cleaned his ailing master. Viola had to do less, no doubt, since her master was vigorous, but Shakespeare wants us to visualize some of the things she must have done: a vessel brought, a pause of waiting, a vessel

taken away. This trivial sacrifice (but it is a proof of the
Duke's sensitivity that he brings it to mind) betokens
sacrifice of real poignancy, which the audience has been
permitted to watch. The Duke has poured out his
secrets to Cesario. All his love for Olivia he has shown
fully and freely, because from a page nothing need be
hid, and because it pleases a man in love to talk about
his desire, and especially when the listener is young and
sympathetic. If it has been pleasure to the girl to listen,
the tale has also been constant pain.

Alive to her master's passion, longing to do him
good, Viola urges his entreaties on Olivia as no previous
messenger has dared. Yet as she presses, her rivalry
intrudes. Shakespeare understands and notates the delicate double process. Instinct teaches her that this is no
time for Castiglione. Courtesies will not pierce Olivia's
ward. Only a tantalizing impertinence—impertinence
and certain words, almost tabu, which a woman knows
will move a woman: 'What I am, and what I would, are
as secret as maidenhead; to your ears divinity, to any
other's, profanation'.[4] With these she wins a private
interview. Maria and the attendants are dismissed.
Olivia has begun to yield. And at Olivia's yielding a
second system of sacrifice, a second system of pathos,
enters the scene, to develop concurrently. Olivia must
sacrifice, above all, her grief for her brother and the
seven years' withdrawal she has sworn; she must also
sacrifice her station; she must sacrifice the dignity of
her sex and take the initiative in wooing.

For a moment she half-repents. She finds an ambigu-
ous phrase to throw the situation into uncertainty; it
may allow her to escape. 'Have you no more to say?'

may be understood by the envoy as an invitation to speak further, but it may be heard as a rebuke and dismissal. All depends on Viola's reaction. And Viola hesitates, then swerves into 'Good madam, let me see your face'. Psychologically perfect: sacrifice and self-indulgence in one gesture. Viola still presses nearer in the knowledge that audacity is the only way to keep alive a parley which, rather than disappoint her master, she will to her own detriment prolong. Yet she asks for herself: like every woman she wants to look at her rival, to read what it is her master loves and she lacks, to read there, too, if she can, a reality that contrasts with her master's illusion. For Olivia it is a shocking challenge. She has promised that her face shall not be viewed for seven years. She cannot agree. She agrees. 'We will draw the curtain and show you the picture'. Viola looks –and praises–praises both for her master's sake and because she loves truth. She pleads again for Orsino, with the classical argument, which Shakespeare has used long since in the sonnets and *Venus and Adonis*, that beauty owes the world its copy; and at Olivia's mockery of that piece of conventional literature, she is incensed and hits back with a rebuke:

> I see you what you are, you are too proud.
> But, if you were the devil, you are fair.
> My lord and master loves you: O, such love
> Could be but recompens'd, though you were
>   crown'd
> The nonpareil of beauty.

Lovely the opportunities to the actress for shifts of thought and tone. Lovely the opportunities for both actresses. It is not only Viola's play. Throughout this

scene the changes in Olivia are wonderful. She speaks
'in starts distractedly'.[5] The boy charms her and hurts
her; the hurt is the more delicious; she is helpless.
Obviously it is not only the Duke who is the masochist,
as his detractors think. It is Olivia, it is everyone else.
It is Antonio, for example, adoring Sebastian so wildly
that he follows him to enemy domain.[6] The play tells
how love inundates its subjects with the pleasure of a
thousand deaths:

> And I, most jocund, apt, and willingly,
> To do you rest a thousand deaths would die.[7]

Only let it be admitted, that Viola has a strong hold on
life amid her sacrifices, which conspire at all points with
the subterranean prosecution of her hopes. The con-
spiracy is wholly unperceived by her. In the language
of our epoch, she 'unconsciously' wills Olivia to fall in
love with her. Pertinacity, winsome impudence, were to
serve her master by enforcing access till Olivia had
heard his suit; but they were also to produce the effect
they produced: the Duke would be secure from Olivia
if Olivia loved a boy. The play's web is spun of sentiment but not of false sentiment. In 'sentimental
comedy' Shakespeare traces the real operation of the
feelings. Here he defines the Janus aspects of sacrifice.
Sacrifice is pure at the conscious level, at the unconscious it is the assertion of the self. This is not to
depreciate it, rather to echo the old wisdom that it is the
true way of gain. Helena in *All's Well*, working no
doubt with a clearer clinical sight, proper to a doctor's
daughter, proves this too.

We may follow the psychological exactitude of

Twelfth Night a little further.[8] Olivia sways between dignity:

> Get you to your lord;
> I cannot love him: let him send no more.

and invitation:

> Unless, perchance, you come to me again,
> To tell me how he takes it.

Left alone, she goes over her visitor's words; dotes; arrests herself: 'not too fast: soft, soft!' The audience is roused to attention by these broken phrases, must guess at the thoughts only half-disclosed: her recollection that she has sworn not to marry, has advertised her oath, must abide by it—'unless the master were the man': unless Orsino's servant, not his master, asked her hand; unless the man would become her master (his bearing shows him fit). Now she has confessed herself. And she accepts the incursion of folly—'Well, let it be'—and sends Cesario her present and the command to return next day. And when next day he comes she takes up her wooing with a woman's mixture of tense pride and impetuous abandonment:

> I did send
> After the last enchantment you did here,
> A ring in chase of you: so did I abuse
> Myself, my servant, and, I fear me, you.
> . . . what might you think?
> Have you not set mine honour at the stake
> And baited it with all the unmuzzled thoughts
> That tyrannous heart can think? To one of your
> receiving
> Enough is shown: a cypress, not a bosom,
> Hideth my heart. So, let me hear you speak.[9]

Viola can only answer 'I pity you'. Cold! And when, after another plea, Viola is still cold, Olivia draws back. A chiming clock—Shakespeare indulges his love of 'noises off'—reminds her of the calls and respects of the world, and gives her momentary strength to behave according to her rank. She again dismisses Viola. But the clock has also told her the late Renaissance tale—that time is fleeting, beauty fleeting. She can't let the boy go, calls 'Stay', holds him in talk, ravished by his very refusal:

> O, what a deal of scorn looks beautiful
> In the contempt and anger of his lip.

Later, after the snubbing she has undergone in those encounters with Viola, it is an incredible surprise to Olivia to find Sebastian pliant in her hands.[10] Shakespeare has brought her to him by a rapid sequence. The clown, seeking Cesario for his lady, finds Sebastian. Sebastian thinks him a pimp and drives him off, but good-naturedly and open-handedly; in fact, with a tip so generous that, when Toby and Andrew burst in with their attack, the clown hurries to fetch Olivia. She drives away her rudesby cousin; fondles Sebastian, panting for his safety; guides him towards the house; and when, to her 'Would thou'ldst be ruled by me', wistfully, yearningly, said because she expects the usual repudiation, he replies 'Madam, I will', she is overwhelmed: 'O, say so, and so be'. To the mere reader this is a typical clinch to punctuate a scene; but it can be exaltation on the lips, in the bearing, of an Olivia transformed.

Sebastian of course does not sacrifice for love. He is fair to Antonio without needing him. He welcomes the bounty and the love of Olivia with good manners, in good faith, and with a blessed freedom of soul. This admission of an exception into the pattern of the comedy is a nice Shakespeareanism. Shakespeare does not want to impose an unreal order on nature. If all who received love in this play had deserved it by their sacrifices, it might seem that love could be earned. But like prosperity it may be a gift, a pearl that has not been sought, not won. In fact there is a light playing about Sebastian and playing in his poetry which represents the grace of luck. For if writers are fascinated by the mysteries of love, they are also beckoned by the mysteries of luck. This is the ancient theme of the fairy-tales. It has some place in Shakespeare. It has perhaps been neglected in our time. Yet one has only to read the opening lines of the well-known story of D. H. Lawrence, 'The Rocking-Horse Winner', to realize what happens when a writer whose roots go down to folk-lore lets his mind work on luck.

* * *

The skein of suggestion is very daintily pulled across *Twelfth Night*. The play says what it means very little by detainable statement; more by its patterns of events, by its pattern of movements as players separate and coalesce; much more by the aural contrasts and dance-patterns of its voices. Among these voices I seem to hear one that is new to Shakespeare: Malvolio's.

We gather from Leonard Digges that Malvolio was originally played, of course so that he *looked* extraordinary in his yellow stockings and cross garters, but also so that he *sounded* extraordinary.[11] The pit and boxes all

were full, says Digges, 'To heare Malvolio, that cross-
gartered gull'. The verb shows that half the comedy of
the character is aural, lying in the things Malvolio says
and the voice in which he says them—a voice Shakespeare already requires in that first sentence of his,
when Olivia asks 'What think you of this fool, Malvolio? doth he not mend?' and gets the violent answer
'Yes, and shall do till the pangs of death shake him'.[12]
It is the ferocious voice of a wracked and vengeful
vanity. And its resonance grows more grotesque when
the forged letter has over-stimulated him, more terrible
when the day in the dark room has maddened him. To
the company assembled at last for all the reconciliations
the Clown reads the steward's petition and mimics the
terrible tone.[13] Olivia jumps in horror: 'How now, art
thou mad?' 'No, madam, I do but read madness: an
your ladyship will have it as it ought to be, you must
allow Vox'. Among the recognizably Shakespearean
voices of good nobleman, good lady, honest seaman,
bright pure girl and bright pure boy, pert wise clown
and pert waiting-woman, here is the new voice. Is
Malvolio's not a Jonsonian voice? And is not Sir
Andrew Ague-Cheek, in name, folly of conduct, and
folly of voice, of pure Jonsonian stock?

It may seem a superfluity to say that the louder and
coarser plot that winds in and out of the elegantly sentimental plot of *Twelfth Night* shows the impress of Ben
Jonson on the older dramatist. From the outset Shakespeare has threaded his court-and-bower comedy with
kitchen comedy. Dromio has played below stairs what
Antipholus has played above. The artisans have con-
verged on the lordlings of *A Midsummer Night's Dream*,

the village constables on the lordlings of *Much Ado.*
But the coarse comedy of *Twelfth Night* has new elements in it. And I suspect they are a Shakespearean
bow to Jonson; and more: that the bow is one of a
series the two writers exchange; significant courtesies;
and yet courtesies only; each goes on his way essentially
himself.

Let us begin with Jonson. He is no practitioner,
probably no friend, of Shakespearean romantic comedy.
Yet there is an early play which is an essay in the genre:
The Case is Altered. Since he did not admit it into his
Folio of 1616, its authenticity has been disputed, but
it is probably his. It has life and charm, and a streak of
power. Perhaps he wrote it in 1597 at a time when he
had resolved that his path to the bays, and for that
matter to a livelihood, must be the path Shakespeare
had taken: he must write for the stage in the dominant
form. What interests me at this moment is, that amid
his adequately twined Plautine material, his pleasantly
adequate handling of the characters and the dialogue,
there are signs that he knew and bore in mind *Two
Gentlemen of Verona* and its plot of the unworthy friend,
and that he had listened to and liked *The Merchant
of Venice.* His Jacques de Prie, 'supposed a beggar',
is a boldly-selective memory of Shylock—Shylock leaving the house with anxiety and admonishment, Shylock crying for his ducats and his daughter. Jacques
de Prie's daughter is not his own, so he cares that much
less for her; and he is a Jonsonian monomaniac, and
cares that much more for his gold; but his manner when
he leaves the house and puts Rachel on guard over the
treasure is printed with the pleasure Jonson felt when

he watched Shylock depart for the Gentile supper.
Shakespeare drew the departure with keen authenticity:
'Perhaps I will return immediately', said Shylock, having no intention of doing so, but hoping to keep Jessica
fearfully vigilant in case he should:

> Perhaps I will return immediately:
> Do as I bid you; shut doors after you:
> Fast bind, fast bind;
> A proverb never stale in thrifty mind.[14]

Jonson varies the instructions but gets a similar voice
and goes after the same psychology. To Rachel, whose
very name seems a consequence of the Biblical associations that the parable of Jacob and Laban set vibrating,
the miser confides the care of his house. First he tells
her to lock herself in; then is terrified that the locked
door will tempt thieves; changes the plan and tells her
to sit in the open doorway

> and talke alowd
> As if there were some more in house with thee:
> Put out the fire, kill the chimnies hart,
> That it may breath no more then a dead man.
> The more we spare, my child, the more we gaine.[15]

Jonson is already himself even amid the old-fashioned
romantic plot. The liveliest sketching in this play is
already humour-sketching: the miser returning to his
hoard of stolen gold, rhapsodizing over it, burying it in
horse-dung for its better safety. And the poetry? That
too is already in Jonson's own style: muscular forward-
thrusting blank verse, the imagery crowding and bub-
bling like flotsam of a flooded city along its stream. And
yet there are faint echoes of Shakespeare. When Angelo
justifies himself in stealing Rachel, whom his friend

had confided to his trust, there is some memory of the *situation* in *Two Gentlemen*; but the *verse* ignores the Shakespearean quibbling of Proteus' soliloquy; instead it borrows the rhetoric of Shylock's great speech of self-justification ('Hath not a Jew eyes? . . .'):

> S'bloud am not I a man?
> Have I not eyes that are as free to looke?
> And bloud to be enflam'd as well as his?
> And when it is so, shall I not pursue
> Mine owne love's longings, but preferre my
> friends?[16]

But the delight with which Jonson responded to *The Merchant* can perhaps best be shown by the fact that in 1599, when he had dropped sentimental comedy for the humours, he still felt pulsing, and subscribed by the flattery of imitation to, some of its felicities. 'Blest be the houre', gloats Sordido in *Every Man Out*,

> Blest be the houre, wherein I bought this booke,
> His studies happy, that compos'd the booke,
> And the man fortunate, that sold the booke.[17]

To Portia, tormenting him for the disappearance of the ring, Bassanio had pleaded:

> If you did know to whom I gave the ring,
> If you did know for whom I gave the ring
> And would conceive for what I gave the ring
> And how unwillingly I left the ring,
> When nought would be accepted but the ring,
> You would abate the strength of your displeasure.[18]

And Portia had answered with the same irresistible pattern. In Shakespeare the flourish is used to add to the poignancy of the game of love, one character talking in good and urgent sadness, the other with a show of

nagging and the hidden fun of rôle-playing and hus-
band-taming. In Jonson, in accordance with his own
style of new comedy, the flourish is perverted to a gro-
tesquerie: his men speak with the voices of the virtuous
and the sentimental to address that which should not be
loved: they expend passion on absurd objects. In the
mouths of his caricatures, poetry and its figures take on
a monstrous beauty: 'a monstrous beauty', as Flecker's
Caliph says, 'like the hindquarters of an elephant'.[19]

But when Jonson was still writing *The Case is Altered*
or had recently finished it, *Henry IV* burst on London.
It is, of course, one of several miracles of Shakespeare's
progress, his sudden ascent to a new level at which he
creates a new mode of English theatre. There has been
a sudden coalition of two arts which Shakespeare has
been practising in separate compartments of his mind:
the art of the political chronicle and the art of comedy.
And what he had thought easy, but embarrassingly
easy, and to be curbed in his comedy, the thunderous
and gross, now came to him as the most significant
component of the new form. The coarse plots of his
comedies turned into the tavern scenes of *Henry IV*, and
took a place in the panoramic design by which the
English nation was presented and brought to judgment.

We know that Jonson, for all his reservations about
Shakespeare, enjoyed Falstaff: he used his name as the
last word of the epilogue of *Every Man Out*,[20] to win a
parting laugh and a complaisant warmth from the
crowd. I suspect that the Falstaff scenes of *Henry IV*
helped more than any other single factor to give Jonson
a glimpse of the comedy in which he might excel: city
comedy, especially City of London comedy; a comedy

of extravagant characters, monstrous in feature and dress, torrential and ridiculous in speech. In Falstaff he saw Shakespeare using energy without sentiment: a criminal energy which justifies itself by appeal to the law of survival. Falstaff alone might not have been wholly sufficient to put him on the way to his humour personae. But he saw him surrounded by other vivid figures, representing follies or corruption from which men commonly suffer yet representing them in incredibly accentuated degree: Justice Shallow, an old man torn between tittering memories of his student exploits and the news of cattle prices in the neighbouring markets; Pistol, driven mad by the theatre. The conglomeration of caricatures taught Jonson his opportunity.

I do not want to seem to limit Jonson's genius to the theatre of humours. He had other gifts, other interests. He longed to make the men and women of Rome walk on his stage and speak in English the words, unforgettable to him, the perfection of human utterance, that they had spoken in Latin. He tried; and the audience cried the plays down, or yawned them down.[21] He rejoiced to exhibit his language in lapidary lyrics and opulent discourse (as he does when Volpone assaults Celia).[22] With these he won the fidelity of the judicious few, the 'Tribe of Ben'. But his great success was the imaging of folly and obsession and whatever is freakishly overgrown in physique, dress, vocabulary, manners, passion. Jacques de Prie was a first draft of the obsessive on the hints of Plautine comedy and Shakespearean tragi-comedy. Then his images were summoned in their plenitude by Shakespeare's Eastcheap.

With Eastcheap or with Shallow's orchard Shakespeare filled three or four scenes of a play. Jonson filled a play. He lost a great deal by that. For it is when Shakespeare's characters are juxtaposed with very different characters that they take and confer their richest meaning. Jonson could not attempt Shakespeare's study of the English nation, scrutinizing its religions, its classes, its professions, its friends and enemies—the major Elizabethan opus. But he was confident that, by the abundance of his invention, the fullness of his language, the force of his predication, he could write other work, which was his and only his, with a cast of none but citizen grotesques. His freaks fill the play because, he implies, they fill the world. He reveals, magnified, the universal experience. Who is not a monomaniac or a fool?

From the 1597 entertainment at the Boar's Head Tavern he embarked on his fabulous voyage, applied himself to the composition of *Every Man in his Humour*.[23] The Lord Chamberlain's men read it; legend says that Shakespeare espoused it; they presented it in the late summer of 1598, Shakespeare playing a principal part. In at least one respect it captured the town: the Jonsonian 'humour' became a byword. He pursued his triumph with *Every Man Out of his Humour*, which the Lord Chamberlain's men gave in 1599 (Shakespeare is not named among the principal actors this time).

Now it was Shakespeare's turn to recognize the other writer's discoveries, and borrow and build with them. When he worked on *Henry V* in the spring (shall we say?) of 1599 he brought in Nym and his chatter of humours for every occasion. In the heat of battle Nym remembers humours as the hummers fill the air from

smoky muskets.[24] Fluellen, Jamy, and Macmorris
bristle with energetic Jonsonian talk. Fluellen's hobby,
the military historians, and his stance, 'a little out of
fashion',[25] might fit well in a Jonson figure. On the
other hand, Fluellen's soundness, the 'care and valour'
of this Welshman, are in Shakespeare's own mode:
beauties of character, not follies.

It was not that Shakespeare was deficient in energy
and needed Jonson's. The energy of Petruchio and
Bottom had been enough for his needs once he had
grasped, by one of those psychic shifts of vision that
come on an artist, that it *might* be turned to the purposes
of *Henry IV*, and *how* to turn it. But an artist alert to his
craft is properly carried into some measure of emulation
of new achievement. Iris Murdoch indicates the process very nicely when she describes how Jake suddenly
saw his potentialities under the net of Jean Pierre's
prize novel. The more extraordinary figures of *Henry V*
are clearly Shakespeare's salute to Jonson. It is possible
that the influence of Jonson has also been at work in
All's Well. At least it has added nuances to Parolles.
'France', Parolles says:

> France is a dog-hole, and it no more merits
> The tread of a man's foot: to the wars![26]

The 'dog-hole' sounds like a Jonsonism. A minute
later Parolles asks Bertram 'Will this capriccio hold in
thee?' Juniper in *The Case is Altered* had appropriated
the same word: 'caprichious' – 'Stay, that word's for
me'.[27] The registration of the parasite's affected energy
in the jerkiness of the metrics is a Shakespearean device,
not a Jonsonian – not, at any rate, at this period of
Jonson's career. But the fatuous vocabulary and, more

generally, the hyper-accentuation of his folly, are Jon-
sonesque. And then: Jonson's influence is thoroughly
at work in *Twelfth Night*. It corruscates in Sir Andrew,
the imitation of Jonson's craven fops; in Malvolio, who
goes beyond imitation and foretells the grand solitaries,
like Morose, whom Jonson will one day create; in the
method of the backstairs plot—the riot of folly let loose,
folly chastised.

Shakespeare has in fact paid Jonson the homage of
blending the Falstaff tankard manner and its anti-
Puritan ideology with the Jonsonian display of monomaniac and fool, and the austere Jonsonian concept of
the farce of folly and punishment.

Punishments and rewards were part of the Tudor
theatrical tradition. 'Some shall be pardon'd, and some
punished', we are told at the end of *Romeo*. But in
Jonson there are few pardons; he is the resolute puni-
sher. 'We hunt not for mens love but for their feare',
Dekker makes him say in *The Untrussing of the Humor-
ous Poet*.[28] He has wormwood wreaths for his sufferers.
Kitely, compulsively tied to his wife, unable to leave
the house for two hours in case she takes advantage
(which, apparently, she has never thought to do), might
be pitiable as well as ridiculous; but to Jonson he is only
ridiculous.[29] The miserable as well as the pretentious
must pay for their maladaptations. If they answer that a
humour is like Cyrano's nose or Gloriana's membrane,
something they are born with,[30] therefore no crime and
not to be expiated, he replies that the comparison is
false: that a humour is something they may get 'out' of,
either because they spontaneously see their errors or are
whipped out—as they step 'out' in 1599. It is not well

that he trounces the unlucky and compulsive as well as the wilful. But he sticks to his position and makes himself Cato the Censor. What we welcome in Shakespeare, by contrast, is an effort—not sustained all along the line, though perhaps it is in tragedy rather than comedy that he hovers towards the morality of expiation—to get beyond the lust to punish. Shakespeare sometimes forgives or tolerates. Planning the Malvolio sequence in Jonson's shadow, he adopts the Jonsonian plan of punishing. Malvolio's despotism is so overweening, his 'humour of state' so pretentious,[31] that it deserves a putting-down, a 'physic',[32] which comes, not in Toby's muscular form of a beating, pistolling, or cudgelling, but in subtler and crueller torments of the egoistic mind after its Luciferan fall. The pursuit of this punishment is as steady and elaborate as Jonson, the clever contriver, could have wished. But there is still, beyond the painful fooling and its peculiar satisfactions, a breath of compassion, for which Jonson has insufficient place. 'Alas, poor fool, how they have baffled thee!' Olivia does not take the view that Malvolio has been suitably punished. Instead: 'He hath been most notoriously abused'.[33] It is her own happiness that would have him happy; but not only that; she has rejoiced to regulate her house with discretion and justice (Sebastian is her witness);[34] she is offended with the brawlers who have disturbed her people; and she would have peace restored. The Duke concurs: 'Pursue him and entreat him to a peace'. So Shakespeare's Jonsonian excursion ends, after all, in a Shakespearean outcome.

* * *

There was at least one more episode in the procession
of give-and-take between Shakespeare and Jonson; and
the differences in their disposition and achievement
show in it as sharply as ever. It is the affair of the
wouldn't-be duellists. The discomfiture which Viola
and Sir Andrew suffer in *Twelfth Night* were some eight
years later remembered and re-created by Jonson in *The
Silent Woman*.

By the middle of the fourth act of *The Silent Woman*
Jonson has everything ready for the springing of his
final surprise. Almost too ready. He needs additional
material to postpone the climax. Daw and La-Foole are
at his disposal. They have been following and pestering
the women with their suggestive but merely teasing
chatter; and they are in the way of Dauphine, to whom
True-Wit has vowed a conquest of all the females in one
fell swoop; they must be dealt with, and True-Wit
makes up his mind to disgrace them. After the *Twelfth
Night* pattern he intercepts each separately, tells how
the other is vengeance-bound; asked to mediate, he
inveigles each into accepting a punishment. Absurd
spectacle, which the ladies are summoned to witness!
Daw is sentenced to five kicks. Amazed at the lenient
award—he had almost expected to lose his teeth—he
begs for six. So: 'give him six, & he will needs'. La-
Foole 'takes a blow over the mouth, *gules*, and tweakes
by the nose, *sans nombre*'. Jonson has been exuberantly
filling time—and it is remarkable how much time he has
managed to fill by squeezing the possibilities of True-
Wit's interviews with the victims. Now he very deftly
dovetails the embellishment into the main plan and
makes it contribute to the climax. He perceives that

each craven will madly respect his supposed chastiser
and feel obliged, in a spirit of adjutancy, to support
every braggart claim the other makes. By the dynamics
of enthusiastic assent, they witlessly force each other
to slay Epicoene's reputation:

La-Foole: Sir John had her mayden-head, indeed.
John Daw: O, it pleases him to say so, sir, but Sir
            Amorous knows what's what, as well.[35]

So when Epicoene finally lifts his skirt and discloses his
boyish contours, these ninnies, already punished under
the Jonson code, are punished again; and this triples
the climax, for in the same discovery, Morose is saved
from a wife and blackmailed into a settlement, and the
Collegiate Ladies are thrown into confusion by the
thought of the 'mysteries' they have opened (a scurvy
Jonsonian touch) to their supposed fellow-female.[36]

Jonson of the epoch culminating in *The Silent Woman*
is generally recognized as the great master of plot integration. In *Twelfth Night* the integration of the 'duel'
with the process of confusion and discovery is equally
ingenious, closer, perhaps more 'necessary'. It begins as Toby's prank with Andrew and Viola, in which
the bully means nothing worse than fleecing both parties
for bribes to avert the contest. Then it heightens step
by step. Shakespeare complicates it,[37] and drives up
Toby's mood from jest to rage, by ringing the changes
on the twins. Antonio rushes to 'Sebastian's' rescue and
has his purse denied by Viola. Toby is incensed at
Antonio's interruption and disgusted at Viola's un-
generous denial, and even Andrew is disgusted and,
seeing an easy opponent, finds his courage. They fall on

their prey—but this time it is Sebastian. And here Shakespeare mixes excitement and farce; he gains much by this varying of the emotional content of the tussle from phase to phase as it evolves. Andrew swipes at Sebastian and is knocked down. Toby grips Sebastian from behind, has him overpowered, then is thrown by a wrestler's trick. He is up, all rage, and out come swords; but at this moment the clown brings Olivia to part them. Toby is now roaring for revenge. Shakespeare does not let us see the last battle; he lets us see the consequences; but holds the disclosure till the crucial moment. Cesario stands arraigned, claimed and reproached by Antonio and Olivia, cleaving to her angry Duke, as beautiful to her in his anger as she in her anger once was to Olivia—cleaving to him as her fixed point in an enigmatic, an apparently distraught, world. Into this tense pageant stumble Andrew and Toby calling for a surgeon; and after them walks Sebastian to tender his apologies to Olivia, and to the confrontation with his lost twin. The subordinate action which has step by step interpenetrated the main action now completes it. Part of the total gratification of the audience in the final scene is the defeat and punishment of the prankster.

The bully is punished. Here we have a punishing Shakespeare. Yes, but the punishment of a spoiler appeals more pleasantly than the punishment of the harmless Daw and La-Foole. In Shakespeare the bully who tars on the timid gets the bangs. In Jonson the plaguing bully gives the bangs and calls them morality.

Presumably Jonson did not see his instruments of justice as bullies, though they were. He saw them as young bucks, and was pleased at the sight, liked them and appointed them legislators, attorneys, hangmen. Come to *Every Man in his Humour* for the first time in your life, and after an act or two you will enquire of yourself, 'These brash young gallants, who get the better of their seniors in these early moves, is Jonson planning a tumble for them in due course?' Then a suspicion grows that he means them to carry the day. And it's too true; he manipulates the plot entirely in their favour. Perhaps you explain the event in terms of his age: 'He was 25. He took the part of his own generation'. But at 35 or 36 he still took True-Wit's part. It is odd. And equally odd, and a folly of the *Essay of Dramatic Poesy* (the most 'persuasively' written of all discussions, yet it delights without persuading), is Dryden's approval of the 'gaiety, air, and freedom' with which Jonson has 'described the conversation of gentlemen in the persons of True-Wit, and his friends'.[38] Dryden saw the victory of the gallants as a victory for himself and that company in which, as the horizon of guns faded down the river, he agreeably discoursed of culture. A tradition runs from Well-Bred to True-Wit, and on to the Restoration bucks ('flown with insolence and wine',[39] says their foe, the great Malvolio of their time in his dark room), and on across another eighty years to Peregrine Pickle and his highhanded coterie, and across another six generations to Basil Seal. But, as I have suggested on another page of this book, a different tradition of the gentleman runs concurrently from Shakespeare through Matthew Bramble to Major Dobbin and Major Tietjens, and it requires modesty rather than wit, decency rather than sophistication, benevolence rather than punishment. It might be said that Shakespeare is middle-class: that the middle-class sensibility is flattered when Toby roars for a surgeon, whereas an upper-class sensibility is flattered when Kitely is tormented, Daw humiliated, Morose tricked. But the class question blurs the view. Cutting through the classes, there is a sentimental sensibility and a ruthless sensibility. In their comic theatre Shakespeare and Jonson divide, and Shakespeare cultivates the first, Jonson the second.

The difference is the less reconcilable if we think of Shakespeare's celebrated heroines, and of Jonson's equally celebrated want of heroines. Shakespeare's best gentlemen are women. Of course he knew all that was to be known about the ferocity of Queen Margaret, the frailty of Cressida, the lust of Goneril and Regan, the destructive love of Lady Macbeth (for it *is* love; she was ambitious for her husband, not for herself; but should have loved his honour more!) Free to indulge, because he used that knowledge, he drew across his comedies a Dream of Fair Women which is, more exactly, a Dream of Intelligence. 'Let me give light, but let me not be light'.[40] If she mitigates it with a gentle wit, Portia's aspiration is the purer, her will the firmer; and it might be uttered by the Princess of France or Rosalind. Shakespeare had eyes and instinct, and was on good terms with his inner forces. The softness of women and the strength to change life were the same for him. For Jonson only manliness was strength. In his poems there are rare moments when he makes a beautiful obeisance to women. There are many moments when he attacks their cosmetics, wigs, con-

traceptives, as if he would sweep every dressing-table,
every bed, into the burning pit. It took some close experience to know as much about women as he managed
to hate. He was always curious about them. He pried
into the married lives of acquaintance, took sides in
husband-wife disputes, loved women, including the
wives of acquaintance. He knew and loved, but was
angry. He could not accept the Queen within, was not
on good terms with his inner forces. His editors, Herford and Simpson, who have reported and appraised
him so massively and so justly, have missed him in one
particular: he was not neurotic, they say;[41] whereas it
is clear that the man who lay awake all night staring at
his big toe and seeing armies of Tartars and Turks,
Romans and Carthaginians, in battle around it,[42] was a
neurotic. He was a neurotic who marvellously organ-
ized his hyperaesthesia into art. It was a part of his constellation that when he made love he preferred to lie in
a voluptuous, endless delay, never to consummate; part
of his constellation to invent fantastics and then to
chastise them for the madness he lent them; part of his
constellation to project women in their most erratic,
irascible, affected, oestrous vein.

Having said this, which is mainly true, I have to concede an exception. Where he admits a heroine into a
comedy he will allow her one virtuous situation: she
may fight against an assailant. Rachel defends her virginity against Angelo.[43] Celia, who, first bullied, then
prostituted by her jealous husband, might reasonably
consent to Volpone resists him and appeals, with a sensibility that reminds us how Jonson kept the Catholic
communion for ten years, to the saints and martyrs.[44]

But he brings little psychological detail to these occasions. They are acts of virtue without the vibration of humanity and without charm.

Whereas Shakespeare sets on his sentiment now this glint of naturalism, now that glint of mythology. In *All's Well*, for example, when Helena offers the King of France the torture of her body, the searing of her 'maiden's name', should she fail to cure him,[45] we discern that the magic of virginity will support her father's science; her earlier conversation with the rude Parolles takes on vital meaning. A similar notion radiates through *Twelfth Night* and meshes with the imagery of 'enchantment'. The lines in which Viola beguiles Olivia by the evocation of maidenhead, send out into the play a hint of the mythic force a virgin wields: a force by which she wins Olivia and eventually will win the Duke.

Jonson's doctrine of manliness is related to his practice of ruthlessness. Rich though he is in lore, he has no faith in magic. Womanly sentiment will do nothing, he thinks, to change the monsters we are into the 'men'[46] – the human race – we should be. The change can only be brought about by manly force, ruthlessly applied. He throws himself into the struggle: the controlled surge of his metres, his giant prose with its profusion of hair and muscles, are directed to subdue the monsters and evoke man. It is a Herculean effort, and might seem completely to justify him. But a problem of all art underlies the nobility of the posture: the artist loves the terrible material on which he works. Jonson loves his monsters. As long as they exist they sanction his brooding, his summons, his tribunal, the violence of his torture-chamber. More than that, he loves them for themselves, loves their absurd and hideous distortions. Shakespeare is caught in a similar trap. He loves the tangle in which his characters go astray; he loves error, muddle, and confusion. They sanction his strange ata-vistic skills of magic and chant and his modern sensi-bility of pardon. He loves them because they provide his occupation. But he also loves them for themselves —'Lord, what fools these mortals be!'[47]—and would hardly wish his magic to change them.

The latent (not the overt) ideology of Shakespearean comedy is much nearer to the liberal and democratic ideology of our day than Jonson's; and consequently we are apt to make Jonson the loser in every compari-son. Perhaps in any day he will be the loser, so much the more various is Shakespeare. It may help to correct the scales if we try to imagine a line or two of tribute that Shakespeare might have written if Jonson had died be-fore him. We must not take it for granted that Shake-speare would have praised the qualities we praise. Con-sider what he chose to praise in Marlowe when he quoted him in *As You Like It*: 'Who ever loved that loved not at first sight?'.[48] Who could ever have con-jectured, had the 'Dead shepherd' dialogue not come down to us, that Shakespeare prized the sentimental wit in Marlowe? I have sought a touch of Jonson in *Twelfth Night* because it helps us to see what he ad-mired in Jonson of the nineties. But what Jonsonian scenes, what wild images, or what to us untypical de-light, reverberated in his mind in the last Stratford years?

Puzzle of Flattery

A professional writer 'studies his market'. That is the
gritty consideration with which this chapter on *Measure
for Measure* begins. In the last years of Elizabeth the
Lord Chamberlain's players enjoyed the favour of the
Court. When Elizabeth died in March 1603 it was
important for them to win the patronage of the new
monarch. Presumably they lobbied skilfully, for in May
they were adopted as the King's Servants—within ten
days after James' arrival in London from the North.[1]
Their next task was to justify the appointment by pleasing him. As far as we know, opportunities for performance at Court were deferred by the outbreak of plague
which drove the King into the shires, where to his
heart's content he followed the hunt. In the autumn he
was guest of the Countess of Pembroke, who hastily
summoned the Servants to Wilton to entertain him.[2]
Taken unawares, they pulled *As You Like It* from the
files: a play of the sylvan hunt: a good choice. But they
were pressing their chief dramatist for a new play suited
to the King's Majesty in his court and capital. My sup-
position is that *Measure for Measure* is the play Shakespeare supplied in answer. I also suppose that before
Shakespeare settled on his topic and treatment he recon-
noitred the King's tastes in pages where he thought
they could best be discerned: pages of which the King
was author. He scanned the *Basilikon Doron*.[3]

I do not assume that Shakespeare relied solely or
even mainly on books for the mobilization of his ideas;

I imagine that the daily scene erupting around him, the gossip of acquaintances and passers-by, and his memories, helped him just as much; but we have ample reason to think of him as one of the world's deftest exploiters of the printed page. The *Basilikon Doron*, a manual of kingship which James had written for the edification of his young son, and which he had issued privately in only seven copies in 1599, was broadcast in an English reprint when the Scottish successor rode south to occupy Elizabeth's throne. Feeding the nation's curiosity about the new master, it was a best-seller in 1603 and 1604. It would have been surprising if Shakespeare had not glanced at it. And it was in keeping with his habits if he pillaged passages from it, and if he used them in a way no other man would have conceived.

To a man who takes up the royal book today with the themes of *Measure for Measure* in mind, three passages in particular sound relevant. First, the remarks on the adminstration of the law. James, who rejoiced to be the British Solomon, the unfoolable and unexcelled adjudicator, urged his son to learn the control of 'advocates and Clerkes'. How?—'Delite to haunt your Session and spie carefully their proceedings'.[4] That excited an image which fetches back to the chroniclers of Harun-al-Rashid and to Plutarch: of the King who spies on his people for love of them and so penetrates the barrier that divides him from their hopes and anxieties. Shakespeare had already dramatized it in *Henry V*. It appealed to him. Secondly, the remarks on temperance and mercy. Of course James recommended these virtues to his son, but qualified the advice: at the outset of his reign a king should withhold mercy and assure good public order by 'giving the Law full execution against all breakers thereof':

> For if otherwise ye kyth your clemencie at the first, the offences would soone come to such heapes, and the contempt of you grow so great, that when ye would fall to punish, the number of them to be punished would exceed the innocent: and yee would be troubled to resolve whom-at to begin: and against your nature would be compelled to wracke many, whom the chastisement of few in the beginning might have preserved.

Shakespeare had already made himself the poet of mercy, and his disposition, and perhaps the prevailing disposition of his English audience, favoured the rôle, yet he may have been impressed by this passage, which has its force. Thirdly, James took pride in continency and enjoined it on his son:

> And although I know, fornication is thought but a light and a veniall sinne, by the most part of the world, yet . . . Heare God commanding by the mouth of *Paul*, to *abstaine from fornication*, declaring that the *fornicator shall not inherit the Kingdome of heaven*: and by the mouth of *Iohn*, reckoning our fornication amongst other grievous sinnes, that debarre the committers amongst *dogges and swine, from entry into that spirituall and heavenly Ierusalem*.[6]

When poets and adventurers of the mind read a passage in this key they usually punctuate it with ribald comment, and perhaps Shakespeare enjoyed himself; but it supplied him with a hint: his play to please the king might touch on man's war against the flesh.

Casting about for a plot which would bring together a prince controlling his advocates and clerks, a governor imposing justice before mercy, man wrestling with flesh, he determined, as everyone knows, on *Promos and*

Cassandra,[7] a play stiff, awkward, but glinting with possibilities, and exhibiting, in the words of the title-page, 'the unsufferable abuse, of a lewde Magistrate' and 'The vertuous behaviours of a chaste Ladye' and 'the perfect magnanimitye of a noble Kinge in checking Vice and favouring Vertue'. Now he must impose his dramatic order. But in doing so he must keep in view a prime intention, to please his king, his Company's patron: to flatter. Flattery is a crude motive, but poets have found it necessary to their survival throughout recorded time. The corollary is that while they have flattered they have contrived to do their more serious work, enlightening their patrons, even criticizing them, even opposing them, as the interest of the material and their sense of truth have prevailed over their immediate intentions. This double process appears to have come into operation as Shakespeare manipulated the *Basilikon Doron* and Whetstone.

In an age when flattery was a widespread accomplishment, Shakespeare was the adept. *Measure for Measure* shows him ranging the gamut from quiet flattery to fulsome. In the first two lines he makes an obeisance to the King:

Of government the properties to unfold
Would seem in me to affect speech and discourse,

implying, at the performance in Court on St. Stephen's Night, 1604, that one among the gathering is the supreme expositor of the science of government, and no dramatist or actor should presume to speak of it in his presence. (If Shakespeare himself played the Duke, so much the more tactful this preliminary disqualification.) But as the play proceeds, the Duke begins to coalesce with the King. A court audience would be alive to potential resemblances and cooperative in welcoming them, though it would not press for consistency and would forget them if the action of the comedy required —so that identifications in a play of this epoch are likely to be intermittent, now sharp and bright, now in recess. Shakespeare exploits the resemblance between the Duke, probing the administration of the law, and the King, who believed in supervising the law officers, and with its help effects some of his neatest flattery in the quiet style. 'I pray you, sir, of what disposition was the duke?' the Duke asks Escalus, testing him.[8] Escalus, coming through the test impeccably, replies: 'One that, above all other strifes, contended especially to know himself.' By which commendation Shakespeare invests the Duke and the King with a virtue which was in fact his own, a tenacity in Socratic questioning and self-questioning. He makes James not only the British Solomon but the British Socrates. 'What pleasure was he given to?' presses the Duke. Escalus replies:

> Rather rejoicing to see another merry, than merry at anything which professed to make him rejoice: a gentleman of all temperance,

which praises James for the 'temperance' James had praised in the *Basilikon Doron*. Now that Shakespeare has uttered two compliments, the English style of flattery calls for an adroit act of detachment. Here it comes: 'But leave we him to his events with a prayer they may prove prosperous', and actors and audience understand that it is the King himself presiding there whom he will not over-boldly describe further and for whose prosperity he prays.

James is a writer, and Shakespeare, the professional, knows that the flattery to which every writer, and especially the amateur, is most susceptible is the echo of his own composition. If he can filter some of the best material of the *Basilikon Doron* into the play, he will be sure of the royal affection. The most memorable passage is that which he admires reluctantly: the warning against clemency in the year when a monarch must clench the framework of society together. He adopts it for the pivot argument of the scene in which, receiving Isabella for the first time, Angelo rejects her plea for mercy. Angelo tells her:

> Those many had not dared to do that evil,
> If the first that did the edict infringe
> Had answered for his deed . . .[9]

and when Isabella answers, 'Yet show some pity', he points out:

> I show it most of all when I show Justice;
> For then I pity those I do not know,
> Which a dismiss'd offence would after gall. . . .

There James hears his own reasoning. And he does not hear any confutation. We shall miss something of the play if, with that knowledge of the plot and the ending which handicaps us nowadays whenever we go to the Shakespearian theatre, we do not see the merit in Angelo's argument. Though harsh, it is sound. Had Angelo firmly stood by it, equalling it with his integrity, we might, while not loving him, have held him justified.

What Shakespeare goes on to show is that austere arguments are not for frail men. They are for angels. No man deserves the name of Angelo. Like the city of

Vienna, man has his lower half, which is his irritation
and fun, and which may not be extirpated. Now, from
disagreement with the King on the question of severity
as against mercy, Shakespeare is gliding into dispute
with him over the significance of fornication, that function of man's lower half, that frailty which is definitive
of the human condition.

To match the King's insistence that fornication was
not venial and to engage his applauding interest, Shakespeare had begun by inventing a heroine who hated
fornication. It was a promising idea, and the result is
indeed remarkable. But Shakespeare could not like her
and could not make us like her; and, as his play developed, he found that he concentrated on changing
her, or on eliciting the human being from the idealist.
In fact, he found she was not really the heroine until
she changed.

Measure for Measure advances as a series of tests.
Angelo is tested and fails. He has not the integrity
which would sanction his austere code. Escalus, as we
have noticed, is tested and passes most honourably (so
that when the Duke greets him in Act V, 'My old and
faithful friend, we are glad to see you', he says it with
special warmth, for he has *proved* him faithful).[10] The
Provost is tested. Claudio is tested. Even the Duke is
tested when Barnardine refuses to cooperate in the sub-
stitute-execution, and the Duke has to give way or fail—
and gives way. Centrally, Isabella is tested.

She is tested, and at first she fails. She fails in her
battle with Angelo over the monstrous ransom. She rejects his temptation and tells Claudio to prepare for his
death. The critics have long canted about this triumph

of her virtue. It is a disgraceful triumph. Which has more claim on a woman, her virginity or her brother's life? The choice may be an unpleasant one, but there was not much doubt about it for Renaissance man (is there for us?). Whetstone in 1578 had been quite sure of Cassandra's decision: she 'stoops'

> to *Promos* wyll,
> Since my brother injoyeth life thereby. . . .
> My Andrugio, take comfort in distresse,
> Cassandra is wonne, thy raunsome great to paye.[11]

To Shakespeare the choice was so obvious that he did not think it possible simply to put a virginity in the scale against a life. His audience might have risen up in protest if an average Isabella had hesitated to choose her brother's life. He had to take the 'daring' step (it is Bullough who calls it 'daring' for not quite the right reason)[12] of making Isabella a novice on the eve of her vows. With that he succeeded in placing her in a tragic struggle, that is, a struggle between a shame and a shame, in which the protagonist loses either way. But she elects the less pardonable way.

Isabella failed in the Christian duty of self-sacrifice. If the play is to be a comedy in which all ends well, she must be tested again and tested till she passes. The Duke's trick of declaring Claudio dead creates the conditions for a new test. He offers her the prospect of revenge if she continues to accept his direction —

> And you shall have your bosom on this wretch,
> Grace of the Duke, revenges to your heart[13]

—and in her grief and anger she wants measure for measure in the sense of a head for a head. This is another failure. But when it comes to the point, when revenge is at her disposal, will she claim it or will she practice the mercy she once advocated? The Duke does not make the choice easy for her. He is determined that the test shall be rigorous. He emphasizes the case for obduracy:

> Should she kneel down in mercy of this fact,
> Her brother's ghost his paved bed would break,
> And take her hence in horror.[14]

Shakespeare keeps Isabella silent while Mariana sues for mercy and the Duke plays the devil's advocate. It is up to the actress to hold the suspense and imply the tension of the inward struggle. Then, with everything to persuade her to choose wrong, she chooses right.

By living up to the code she alleged to Angelo, she gives validity to it. When she has done that by her free choice, the Duke, the riddling God, can respond by a general 'remission': mercy to all.

Exposing the noble, formidable, unsympathetic character of Isabella, and leading her through a course of decisive change, Shakespeare detects the origin of her problem and indicates it with two terse strokes. In the prison-scene when Claudio tells her he is prepared to die, she congratulates him by a comparison with her father:

> There spake my brother: there my father's grave
> Did utter forth a voice[15]

and then, when Claudio swerves and wants to beg the ransom, she rebukes him by the same standard:

> What should I think?
> Heaven shield my mother play'd my father fair!
> For such a warped slip of wilderness
> Ne'er issued from his blood.[16]

There Shakespeare has implied the explanation of her
resolute chastity and of all her conduct in the play.
Himself a father who 'loved the breeder better than the
male'[17] and was emotionally involved with his daughters, and who at a date probably close to that of *Measure
for Measure* drew Lear and Cordelia, Shakespeare was
sensitive to the relationship of fathers and daughters
and threw around it a fierce, tender, and analytical light.
Isabella's passion for her dead father gives her a dis-
tinctive strength, isolates her from young men, is leading her from the world to the convent. She cannot
think fornication venial. Of all offences she abhors it
most. Therefore her inability to subdue herself to save
Claudio. But when a Father counsels her, she can submit to his guidance. And when the Duke, father of his
kingdom, as he manifests himself by his care throughout the drama, and the incarnation of God the Father,
asks for her in marriage, at last she can yield. It is
entirely credible, despite the critical strife over the matter, that the play ends happily with a troth-plighting
and so with the dissolving of the 'cold' chastity at which,
like Coleridge, we necessarily shudder in the early
scenes.

That final mitigation of Isabella's austerity is vital.
The practice of mercy is closely connected with the
principle of *moderation*. The word 'moderation' inheres
in the title *Measure for Measure*. When Skelton translated the Greek precept, μηδὲν ἄγαν, he used 'measure'
as the most convenient English sign for 'nothing
in excess'. 'In measure is treasure', he wrote in *Speke
Parot*.[18] So if 'measure for measure' implies, following the Bible, 'Get what you gave', and thus raises

the question of justice, and if it implies ,'Let your deeds
come up to your advocacy', and thus tests every idealist,
it also suggests, 'Let moderation be answered by
moderation—let moderation prevail'. If Shakespeare's
plays in any degree adumbrate a doctrine, moderation
is at the heart of it. 'Moderation' comprehends a wise
mercy; comprehends the patience and stability of Horatio, one of Shakespeare's true heroes; comprehends
the tolerance of Lafeu, another man in whom Shake
speare recognizes an approximation to human health,
the tolerance which says to Parolles 'though you are a
fool and a knave, you shall eat'.[19] It recurs in the writ-
ings of the Renaissance, though it is not a Renaissance
attitude, being the obverse of the immense hubris
which was the creative energy of the age. It is utterly
humane, yet it is not Humanist. It is unlike the new
glory of the Renaissance; it is old and seasoned; it
comes down from Dante, from the Middle Ages, from
Aristotle. It is traditional wisdom, the only ripe fruit of
man's experience and speculations. With its judicious
restraint it warns that in our excellence, no less than in
our vices, we must be moderate. Even her cold virtue
Isabella must moderate, if she is to be truly golden. 'In
measure is treasure.' At length assenting to the golden
doctrine she will lay down to the father-king the trea-
sures of her body.

The tone of Lafeu and the texture of *All's Well that
Ends Well* are, in an obvious way, adapted to a com-
mon-sense doctrine. The texture of *Measure for Measure*
is different, strange. It is shot with theology and meta-
physics. This drama is, as some of its twentieth-century students have agreed with excitement, a Morality,

a Theatre of the World. It is Shakespeare's *Paradise Lost*. It is his attempt to show how God is misunderstood and to justify Him. We complain of the evils of our existence. God, in the person of the Duke, feigns to concede that he has been too lax, has allowed riot and imperfection. He will withdraw and let some better, sterner genius correct His mistakes. All to show that the better, sterner way would not be better: it would deny man his humanity, and, doing that, would deny God the exercise of mercy, which is His crowning beauty and pleasure, and which man should imitate.

Shakespeare followed his thought to its conclusion— and the further he went with it the more deeply he ran into difficulty and perhaps danger. He had meant to propitiate King James by filling his ear with flattery, and especially with the echo of his own words. But the quizzical Stratford mind had found it impossible to use the most striking passages without analysing, doubting and retorting. The end-result: a picture of the world and a mirror for magistrates and kings which, in effect, criticized James' administration. During his first months on the throne James had practised the rule of initial severity which he enjoined on his son. He had hanged the cutpurse at Newark, huff-snuff.[20] He had hurled his thunderbolt at Raleigh;[21] arrested him promptly; saved him from death, it is true, but under cruel circumstances; was holding him in prison as a perpetual warning of the dreadful power under the Stuart affability. *Measure for Measure* deplored the procedure. There is a passage in the play which, once we have begun to think in these terms, makes us jump: Claudio, explaining his arrest, guesses that Angelo is taming the public as if it were a horse and he a rider:

> Who, newly in the seat, that it may know
> He can command, lets it straight feel the spur ...[22]

It may be that, by a familiar psychological sequence, the very task of flattering provoked an unconscious reaction in Shakespeare and certain images such as this, hazardous beyond the requirements of his drama, rushed in.

But I would not include among the hazardous speeches those with which the debauched Lucio criticizes the Duke.[23] Although the play encouraged the King to see himself in the Duke, the slanders, however free and gross, were not likely to give him offence. They occur within a favourite situation of the comic stage: authority, disguised, hears itself censured with a liberty no one normally dares take. Generally speaking, the gambit may work in either of two ways: the censures may be justified, the ruler hear home-truths; or they may be sheer fiction, and the audience may relish the exchanges because a fibber and braggart is preparing his own catastrophe when he shall be called to account. The second is, clearly, the method in *Measure for Measure*. The actor who plays the Duke has already had the opportunity to prove him, if enigmatic, unmistakably noble, pure, concerned for the people; and, to make assurance doubly sure, the testimonial of the reliable Escalus follows Lucio's inventions. James would be the first to recognize and relish the comedy, appropriate in a court with its usual contingent of braggarts, know-alls, and whisperers. It would please his pride in his own shrewd insight into human foibles. He would mutter how he knew a score of Lucios, the gallants who affected one thing to his face, another behind his back;[24] and next moment he would hear Shakespeare confirming his thought:

> No might nor greatness in mortality
> Can censure 'scape; back-wounding calumny
> The whitest virtue strikes. What king so strong
> Can tie the gall up in the slanderous tongue?[25]

A little later, to fill the moment in which Isabella and Mariana concert their arrangements, the Duke repeats this 'sentence'; brooding and moralizing, he repeats it more elaborately;[26] Shakespeare invokes words of number, words of volume, words (like 'dream') that conquer time, and so performs an illusionist's trick of elongating the mere moment of the ladies' withdrawal, and a poet's trick of infusing a comment on the petty world of everyday affairs with the sense of the divine and the eternal. The 'sentence' and all the shifts which have led to it contribute to the total result, in which a play intended as a flattery, and laden with flattery, becomes a major act of interpretation of life. Shakespeare transcends his flattery, transcends his purposes. So a poet often does. He starts with trivial or deplorable intentions and moves through them to soaring discoveries.

But if the shrewd king taxed him with dissent on that hazardous issue of the royal mercy, what could Shakespeare say to clear himself? He could profess that he was intent solely on one lesson, that of moderation; and that he had derived it from the *Basilikon Doron*. James, linked by his Scottish education and his innate conservatism with the Middle Ages, constantly used the terminology of the old scholarship, and had advised

Prince Henry: 'Even in your most vertuous actions, make ever moderation to be the chiefe ruler.'[27] By reference to that, the supple Shakespeare might evade complaints. And it may be that he felt entirely secure in the identification of the monarch with God, which is at once the play's most brilliant move, transforming the comedy to a Morality, and its most fulsome flattery. 'Your Grace', acknowledges Angelo, has watched everything 'like power divine'.[28] James would not blench at the identification. The *Basilikon Doron* points out that the King, though he is God's servant, is also, by virtue of his heritage and responsibilities, the reflection of God. The sonnet on the first page of his book begins

> God gives not Kings the stile of *Gods* in vaine
> For on his Throne his Scepter doe they swey

and closes

> And so ye shall in Princely vertues shine,
> Resembling right your mightie King Divine.

Of course, there is this to be said for Shakespeare's exploitation of the King's sense of divinity: that if he wished the law to be administered more mercifully, it was as well to infuse the King with the feeling that he was the merciful God. Like all good counsellors and clever propagandists, Shakespeare had to make it seem, even while he was arguing with the King, that he was echoing the King's own arguments, reiterating a conception of clemency learned from his example.

There is a sense in which the play probably failed in 1604. A peculiar style distinguishes it, a style announced immediately in the first two lines with their inversion and their abstractions, a style deliberately speculative. A style deliberately desiccated, too, re-

lieved of 'music', for James had canny suspicions of the
art which

> oft hath such a charm
> To make bad good, and good provoke to harm.[29]

Accepting the fashionable myth that James was a
Solomon, dedicated to the abstruse, Shakespeare had
thought that a new poetry, a schoolman's poetry, would
be to the royal taste. But he never again used the style.
It must have gone unappreciated. Apparently he had
misunderstood his patron. But thank goodness for the
misunderstanding and the stylistic excursion it promp-
ted. The unusual diction and rhetorical organization
make the play Shakespeare's Dry Miracle. And of
course there is implicit in the very misunderstanding
one of those paradoxical consonances which are sometimes the delight of literature: Shakespeare tells us in
the play that the King is misunderstood, and he himself misunderstood the King in formulating a style to
please him.

The Spanish Ambassador, Gondomar, was later to
construe the King better and entertain him with horse-
play. Shakespeare, when eventually he knew a little
more of James, moved in the same direction. If the
witches of *Macbeth* are adapted to the taste of a king
who preened himself on his insight into witches real
and false, their antics and incantations are adapted to
his foible for the obviously grotesque. But more interesting is Ben Jonson's counterblast to Shakespeare's
Morality Play. His comedy of *Bartholomew Fair*, produced before the king in 1614, dramatizes authority
spying on the people in the name of justice, borrows
Mistress Overdone's name for the respectable but not

irreproachable Justice Overdo, congregates cutpurses and bawds all as seamy as Pompey and Froth. But it is in one great essential unlike *Measure for Measure*. Instead of a metaphysical Theatre of the World it offers a hurly-burly, common-level Fair of the World. In the name of good sense and good order the classical, authoritarian Jonson refused to trespass on the things that were Caesar's or on the things that are God's. He loved Shakespeare. But he feared that his friend sometimes presumed, wildly presumed: presumed in *The Winter's Tale* and *The Tempest* 'to make nature afraid' with theatrical effects beyond the scope of theatre;[30] presumed in *Measure for Measure* to affright Nature and society with matters beyond the scope of a playwright. He thought Shakespeare, in the very play of moderation, immoderate.

One point might be added. A topic touched, however lightly, by these notes is the influence of the Stuart newcomers on the Elizabethan drama, and the changes they encouraged. Any extensive consideration of this subject would have to take account of Anne of Denmark, who was a more important influence than her husband. *Measure for Measure* and *Macbeth* are cases where we can watch Shakespeare aiming directly at the King. But they are exceptional. There are, however, one or two cases where we may think that, while the writer's main concern was to furnish a play for Anne, he kept a weather-eye on the King, whom he tried to attract with a pass or two. *Othello* may have been such a play: designing it for Anne, he garnished it with allusions to those eastern enemies whom James never tired of discussing, and, to prepare himself, glanced at the King's

poem on Lepanto, celebrating the defeat of the 'circum-
cized Turband Turkes'.[31]

If *Measure for Measure* was not quite the right play
for James, perhaps *Othello* was not quite the right play
for Anne. It is no use aiming the most wonderful
arabesques in English rhetoric at a foreign lady whose
grasp of the language is small. Anne was theatre-struck,
but her English entertainers could more easily flatter
her eye than her ear. When that was appreciated, the
masque became the mode at Court, and there followed
that modification of the London theatre at large, of
which something will be said in another chapter.

* * *

A postscript. When the foregoing commentary was
already in print in *The Shakespeare Quarterly*, I saw the
Bristol Old Vic's version of the play, directed by
Tyrone Guthrie. The memoranda that follow were
recorded immediately after the performance while its
revelations were fresh.

(1) The opening of the play: the Duke appears on a
tower-top, the helmets of guards in a ring deep below
him. He looks with the absolute concentration of God.
He is a Kafka God: the authority on his castle. He is
also a Renaissance God: God surveying the universe:
God foreseeing; God resolving to descend, incarnate
himself in a deputy, play the Theatre of the World. He
makes the decision. His features change from absolute
contemplation, which is creation, to the mobile wry
features of the Duke. He steps down, is in the world,
calls out 'Escalus'. Escalus comes to him.

(2) We ask: how can it be that God who foresees

everything does not foresee that Angelo will dishonour
the pact with Isabella and order Claudio's death? How
can God be put to straits by a kink in the pattern? The
answer is: because he made men free, and men can be
more evil than he expected. Or the answer is: that as
God at the height he foresaw all, but that when he takes
on the incarnation he takes on some of man's limitations
with it and must plan and counter-plan in the world's
way. Except: not as corruptly as free man may plan;
but according to his own honour. For example, bound
to God's honour he cannot behead Barnardine when
Barnardine is unready and unwilling.[32] God himself is
tested by that turn in the events.

(3) The scene when the Friar-Duke happens on
Juliet in the prison is one of those short passages with
which Shakespeare breaks up two major sequences,[33]
his main purpose being to mark the passage of time, or
to rest his actors or give them two minutes to change,
but *out of which he always gets additional value*—and so
should the modern director, and so Guthrie does. The
Friar blesses Juliet: makes the sign of the Cross over
her; then makes the sign of the Cross over her womb,
recognizing and hallowing her child. A light of gratitude and happiness flares up on her face. Lovely sentiment! But immediately the Friar dislocates it; strides
to one side; with an almost jovial brutality shouts 'Your
partner, as I hear, must die tomorrow'. She gives a
shriek, collapses. Her shriek shakes the theatre—like
Cassandra's 'Cry, Trojans, cry'[34] in Guthrie's great
Troilus. Is the effect right for this Morality play? Yes,
it belongs to the enigma of the 'old fantastical duke of
dark corners',[35] which is the enigma of God. It belongs

to the seeming capriciousness of God, which is part of his mystery. He seems at once beneficent and brutal—as in those mediaeval Moslem writers who say, when God teases man, 'God laughs'.[36] The contradiction is resolved by the play—to resolve it is the point of the elaborate steps and stresses of the long last scene: we understand that God's world is one in which compassion is to create him in despite of all the reasons he can raise against himself.

(4) Beautiful strokes, naturalistic strokes mixed with allegorical, after Isabella's outburst against Claudio.[37] Horrified by her brother's 'baseness', as she thinks it, in pleading for his life, she reels against the prison wall, hysterical. Everything human seems stained, untouchable; she may refuse to hear a word; perhaps nothing can fetch her back to human contact and coherence. The Friar clears everyone else from the room. There is a silence in which you watch him revolving what words, what tone, can make her listen. He finds them in 'The hand that hath made you fair hath made you good' spoken without fulsomeness, no obvious appeal in them, almost factual, but just enough understanding and thought to reach her—while still leaving it a question for us whether frigid goodness is the best goodness. Then the Friar goes and leans against the wall too. His back to her, he looks the other way. A touch, a memory, of the considering God in his demeanour again. And that makes him the Father; the sense of the Father in him passes to her. Without looking at her he extends his hand, opens it backwards to her, so that, in a sudden impulsive response of trust, she snatches it and holds it tight.

(5) When the Duke is alone to deliver the gnomic lines which are the *clou* of the play—'He who the sword of heaven will bear'[38]—Guthrie has him chant them. They take on their liturgical character. We no longer ask, as the printed page lets us ask, whether as poetry they are too terse. They are sibylline truths.

(6) Angelo, played by Richard Pasco, becomes a fully *tragic* figure: a man *torn* between his passion for purity, or the name of purity, and his obverse passion for flesh; between his knowledge of fundamental decency and his grasping ambition. He knows the best and follows the worst—to his own horror. Of his playing in the first moves of the final scene one might urge in criticism that he looks so guilty (he *feels* guilty, and is demoralized by the feeling) that there can be no margin of doubt: he gulps into his handkerchief at Isabella's accusation, his cheeks are blenched. With an effort he pulls himself together, and tries to bluff the situation out with seeming and lies. But once he understands that 'power divine'[39]—from his habitual low voice he rises at this phrase to a full note of recognition and veneration— has 'looked upon his passes', he welcomes the unmasking, pleads not hypocritically but wholeheartedly for death. Guthrie at this point has the Duke dominating the stage with the serene power of absolute holiness; and Angelo, roused to his genuine capacity for worship, asks for death much as Gerontius contemplating the beauty of paradise wishes for the cleansing pains of purgatory: '. . . Take me away'.[40]

(7) And when in this final scene Isabella defeats God's temptations (for there is no devil in this Shakespearean comedy), refuses the claims of vengeance,

goes down on her knees and supplicates for Angelo's pardon, and so passes the test and justifies God's creative hope of man, a smile of beatitude fills the Duke's face.[41] No one on the stage can see it; they are all bent low in their plea for mercy and their suspense. But the smile flows over the audience, fills the theatre. Then it is withdrawn by the teasing God and a frown resumed that he may complete his Play, reward while he pretends to punish.

(8) The Bristol Old Vic actors underplayed some of the lines, used the low voice often. There were lines that did not carry. But that occasional failing apart, what a beautiful delivery. Immensely rapid, the tempo; and yet the syntax of some of Shakespeare's intricate sentences became crystal-clear: understood and made understandable. In the fierce exchanges between Angelo and Isabella how superbly Shakespeare argues for both sides. We admire the French dramatists, their brains sharpened by the long Lycée tradition, for the power to play the chess of dialogue: against every argument a thwarting argument. But Shakespeare outdoes them. Powerful reason answers powerful reason. In concise language. The sentences look difficult but are beautifully architected; they have only to be defined, as the Bristol Old Vic defined them, by the intelligent voice.

* * *

It will be clear that I have offered two kinds of material in this chapter. There is the historical speculation: that Shakespeare intended *Measure for Measure* to please his new royal patron, studying the 'market' in the *Basilikon Doron*. There is a view of the play as a fusion of naturalism (the portrait of a frigid girl, and the fable of the shock-treatment that warms her to life) and allegory (a Welttheater, a comedy of God and man). The view of the play is not *dependent on* the historical speculation; but if the speculation is true, then the emergence of such a massive play from such banal beginnings throws light on the movements of a poet's mind. Tyrone Guthrie's production does not test, and in the nature of the case no production can, the historical speculation. That still rests what it was, a leap from the springboard of the first known reference to *Measure for Measure*, the Revels Office account of payments to the King's Company for the plays performed at Court during the Christmas holiday of 1604. What Guthrie's production confirmed, as it seemed to me, what it thrillingly confirmed was the view of the play.

An Old Man's Methods: "Henry VIII" and the late plays

Was Shakespeare an 'old man' when he wrote *Henry VIII*? One or two scholars at an Ontario Seminar smiled when I said so—scholars who happened to be 47 or 48 and were at their hard-hitting best. But everybody who comments on the late plays subscribes to one myth or another, and I like the myth that the Elizabethans and Jacobeans did everything earlier than we do: took degrees earlier, married earlier, campaigned earlier, rotted earlier. Indeed, the historian Creighton Gilbert has recently maintained, and fortified the claim with evidence, that the myth is truth.[1] Shakespeare had led a busy existence. It is fair to the facts to call him an old man at 48.

On the evidence of *Henry VIII* and the preceding 'romances', what were Shakespeare's interests and theatrical objectives in the years when he felt himself to be the veteran; when sometimes he despised the newcomers to the theatre and thought himself a Lafeu among Bertrams; when sometimes he felt outstripped and saw himself as the Antony among the boy Caesars; when sometimes he felt a master-artist, a Glendower become a Prospero?

It had been his habit, in the days when he was occupied full-time in the theatre, to set himself with every new play a fresh problem: to make it a matter of pride, as Eliot, working from his example, has made it, not to repeat himself. He might write two plays about a husband consumed by jealousy, but in one he would imagine an unsophisticated man victimized by an adroit enemy and entirely deprived of help, while in the second he would deliberately reverse the conditions and show a man surrounded by friends and good advisers but polluting himself in defiance of them, victim of 'the imposition . . . Hereditary ours'.[2] In *Henry VIII* Shakespeare seems in some respects to have broken his self-imposed rule. Perhaps he decided, when the Players, needing a special work for the marriage of Princess Elizabeth, pressed him for a script under his pension agreement, that he would comply with the least possible exertion. He rapidly drew a play together around a theme he had used before: the evolution of a paternal monarch.

For that is the spine of his last play. At the outset Henry is well-meaning, innately good, but easily fooled. These cardinals trifle with him,[3] so do the aristocratic intriguers. He is duped into the condemnation of Buckingham. He is decoyed into abandoning a good wife. He drops his Cardinal, half decoyed into it, half finding his own way. At last he learns sovereignty. He who was duped into destroying Buckingham is not duped into sacrificing Cranmer. He dominates the intriguers, is master in his own house. He is lonely, but with the loneliness of a king or God, the watcher, the penetrator of motives, the ruler.

But how much more elaborately Shakespeare had graphed the evolution of a king, the father of the country evolving out of a boy ashamed of his father, in the three plays about Hal. Then he was elated by the

theme; the whole conception was a discovery; he presented it in brilliant detail. In 1612, resorting to
a similar interpretation of Henry for no better reason
than to spare himself labour, he presented it con-
cisely.

He at first chafed under the commission to write
Henry VIII and thought it a burden to be discharged as
rapidly as possible. But it is one thing for a writer to
decide to throw a work off carelessly, another thing to
do so. As the drafting went forward, he warmed up to
the material; his interest stirred despite himself. If the
emergence of the king never quite heated him, some of
the material associated with the process did. For example, the description of court-intrigue. Here again he
was on ground he had covered before. The 'convention',
as we say, the convention that a poet's business is to
denounce the vices of the Court went at least as far
back as Skelton, in whose day *Henry VIII* is set. Shakespeare had often used it (and at least once, satisfying his
appetite for change, had deliberately refused it and
imagined Leontes' virtuous retinue). But there is a
bubble of vitality in this last version of it. When he
retired from London life, the experience of the capital
took new shape in his memory. His occupations in the
past had sometimes carried him to the fringes of the
court, and he had seen that there was a good deal of
truth in the literary legend that courtiers, the best and
the worst alike, live destructively on each other's blood.
Now he ruminated on the matter with an old man's
pleasure in understanding human behaviour. He would
make of this play, the greater part of which takes place
in the chambers, galleries, and apartments of the royal

palace, an anatomy of intrigue. There was some difficulty in the plan. The whispering in corridors, pro-
scription in locked rooms, could not be exactly festive,
not exactly a nuptial benediction. Two decades earlier
he had more happily conceived Theseus and Hippo-
lyta, Oberon and Titania, for the wedding they presumably celebrated. It is at once the perfection and the
not-quite-sufficiency of *A Midsummer Night's Dream*
that Shakespeare found no strong conflicting purpose
rising within and against his comedy. The imperfection,
interest, and grandeur of *The Merchant*, *Measure for
Measure*, and *Henry VIII* lie in such a conflict; and in
the long run (that is, for us though not for Shakespeare's
immediate audience) the conflicting purpose prevails
and provides almost all the energy of the occasion.
Shakespeare must have sensed the doubleness of *Henry
VIII* as he worked. But evidently he persuaded himself
that the gradual ascent of the King and the final presentation of the infant Elizabeth, and the support of the
colour of pageantry, would secure his play with the
royal audience.

The doubleness is active in the opening scene. Shakespeare begins with a vivacious flourish, a promise of the
pageantry to come: the story of the Field of the Cloth of
Gold. But at once, with his practised capacity for making everything cooperate in the design which is more
deeply engaging him, he turns the material towards his
study of intrigue. Norfolk is established as the type of
the aristocratic court-schemer. Against him is set Buckingham, another type: the angry man too impetuous to
scheme patiently for the gratification of his anger, therefore doomed to a quick catastrophe. Buckingham's

nearly forty lines on the 'treasonous' self-aggrandizing manoeuvres of Wolsey behind the pageantry of the Cloth of Gold describe the methods of diplomacy and of corruption in Henry's and every age.[4] Grim material, it is raised to the poetry of pleasure by the old ruminating mind that sees flashing behind it the knife-strokes of hard, fighting life. And then, Shakespeare goes on, reading his sources with a sure comprehension of the patterns of deed and consequence, chicanery in foreign relations leads to injustice in home affairs. Queen Katharine, when she comes forward in the next scene to plead for the oppressed people, shows that Wolsey, having been paid by the emperor to break the peace and now richer than ever for the transaction, has in the sequel impoverished and crippled the English commons, financing the war by compelling from each subject 'the sixth part of his substance'.[5] This scene in turn leads to Wolsey's campaign to destroy the Queen. Not that he has wholly lost the encounter with her: while she has prevailed on the King (who, Shakespeare supposes for the purpose of his drama of a man wholly well-meaning but as yet unconscious, knew nothing of the levy) to remit the taxation, the Cardinal has dexterously salvaged something from the affair: 'let it be noised', he tells his secretary,

> That through our intercession this revokement
> And pardon comes.[6]

But he will not forgive Katharine for opposing him and uncovering his exactions to the King. She must go. So, step forcing step with a tragic thrust, there follows the York Place masquing,[7] music-lifted and ever-loosening and verging towards orgy, at which he contrives—or else observes and exploits—the King's encounter with Anne Bullen.

But while the Cardinal, with his limitless ambition and splendour (which also were implied in the tone-setting narrative of the Cloth of Gold) is pushing his schemes on a reckless scale, Norfolk and the nobles are coordinating their schemes against him.[8] He falls. But that is not the end of the intrigue. The nature of the Court, the nature of government, the nature of all administration, whether national or municipal, whether big business or little business or local club, is that when one man falls, another captures his place, and the opposition reorganizes and the intrigues resume. This is the picture behind the shifting events of *Henry VIII*. With enjoyment of the human horror, with enjoyment of his taut skill in dramatizing it, Shakespeare shows ambitious men combining against the favourite of the hour, downing him, splitting, recombining: faction begetting faction, injury begetting injury, as crime led to crime in the early plays of the Roses.

Warmed by the drawing of the clinical picture, Shakespeare risked some last comments on the question it requires: why evil is compounded with good in the human constitution? 'Last comments' in the sense that he had already made several at several points of his career. The question perplexed and provoked him and his contemporaries, to whom it had descended in a peculiar form. The English dramatists of 1600 were children of the Humanists; they would not have been doing their work but for a hundred years of Humanism. The Humanists had presented them with extremes: on the one hand, the conception of man as capable of

everything, endowed with a creative faculty of godlike
stretch, on the other hand, an aversion for the animal in
man. The academics had simply condemned carnality.
It was 'ab-hominable'.[9] Holofernes' derivation, though
false, is significant. The teachers maintained that carnality was in man but not of man, and was to be ignored
or censured or mortified. In fact, the trouble with the
Humanists was that they weren't human enough: they
wanted paragons; they didn't like mere men. 'The
worst part of the human picture,' said Ascham, 'is from
the navell downwards'.[10] Shakespeare was familiar with
this view. Sometimes he lent it to his characters. Sometimes they uttered it in torment:

> But to the girdle do the gods inherit,
> Beneath is all the fiend's.[11]

The dramatists could not ignore sub-navel man. They
insisted on studying him, bringing him nearer and
enlarging him. Therefore that predominant impression
of blood, violence, lust, which the plays of the great
English epoch convey. If they often echo denunciations
borrowed from the Humanists, denunciation is not
really their tendency. Their tendency is to reconcile the
upper and the lower man.

For man doesn't really dislike his lower half. Not
even a Humanist. Not even Holofernes. The daughters
of the parish profit very greatly under him.[12] Constru-
ing Shakespeare's dialogue as Shakespeare intended,
Michael Langham, in a matchless *Love's Labour's Lost*
at Stratford, Ontario, had Holofernes tweak Jacquen-
etta's rear; and his actor tweaked to perfection, switching away with a look that both denied that he'd done it

and watched for the result, Kate Reid's beaming simper of comprehension and consent.

Shakespeare undertook an intricate consideration of Holofernes' problem in *Measure for Measure*, analysing a Deputy, whose name shows that he claims, like the Humanists, to be in action and apprehension an angel, but who falls prey to his abominable weakness. The outcome is a justification of the lower self and the Fall: 'best men are moulded out of faults', if only mercy be granted.[13] This is Shakespeare's version of Milton's 'justification' of God's ways. The last and largest Renaissance attack on the problem was Milton's in *Paradise Lost*. Humanist Milton looked from Ascham's standpoint and Holofernes', and this although he had spent some of his best young days at the London theatre and had learned the management of words and the liberation of the fancy as much from the dramatists who preceded him as from the poets. It is one of the distresses of literature that a master who could take so much power and charm from the stage could not only serve the party that closed the theatres, but fail to take the liberating and healing thought of Shakespeare into his own. Shakespeare's adventures with the problem may seem casual compared with Milton's lifelong attention to it. But the very lightness of a Shakespeare, the suddenness of his turn to a fundamental question from a trivial occasion, is an adventage. Milton had disadvantages: was not free-minded, not flexible; was too ambitious, plotting a book that would be a city, a tower to heaven, and a name; was so enamoured of philosophy that he forgot men, and when he remembered men didn't understand them. It is true that, like every artist,

Milton made a miracle of his disadvantages. But he did
not invent a justification of God as felicitous as Shakespeare's in *Measure for Measure*. Moreover, Shakespeare
was not, in this play or any other, attempting a final
verdict. Milton was—that was his crushing disadvan-
tage. Shakespeare was the artist who undertakes an adventure with an idea, undertakes Durrell's act of play,
adopts a point of view, 'tries it on', enables us to experience the possibilities of it without hazard. Then he has
a go at the problem again with a different hypothesis.

In *The Tempest* Shakespeare invented an amusing
new approach to the Humanists' problem. He imagined
a girl who has been brought up seeing no one but her
father (who's a half-god) and a monster (who's a half-
devil). Suddenly confronted with man, what will she
think? First she sees the Prince. Of course, that's an
easy one:

> I might call him
> A thing divine, for nothing natural
> I ever saw so noble . . .[14]

Later comes the real test: she is shown a collection of
court-intriguers and scoundrels, with the decent old
Gonzalo single among them to indicate the proportion
of good to bad in any human sample. Now what has she
to say? She still likes them:

> How many goodly creatures are there here!
> How beauteous mankind is![15]

Prospero drily comments

> 'Tis new to thee.

Her welcome, with its love of life and its reminder that
that means love of man, including bad men; his aged
scepticism, and the compassion for the illusion of youth

that underlies it: this concatenation, this comedy, brightens the debate, and the brightness is a vote for life. But the old Shakespeare was multiple-sighted, not content to leave us or himself enjoying that pleasant flight of fancy. He simultaneously tried a different adventure with Caliban: there *is* an element of lust and devilry which is beyond society and beyond cure:

> on whose nature
> Nurture can never stick; on whom my pains,
> Humanely taken, all, all lost, quite lost.[16]

In Caliban he rejected the beastliness of man. Not the rascality of man: Stephano and Trinculo, who have no sense of beauty and who have suffered nothing, he tolerated, as nothing worse than clowns and inebriates, and licensed them to recognize and scorn the beastliness or fishiness of Caliban, as if even a fool, even a knave, knows the difference of beastliness and detests it. To modern taste this is not very agreeable, and we struggle against it and claim that Shakespeare half-awares discerned the heroism of the suffering beast: some rights Caliban has and they have been violated, some instinct for beauty has been moved in him but it is thwarted. But perhaps we should be as tough as Shakespeare in trying the feel of dramatized hypotheses. Caliban is one of his hypotheses.

The matter was still vexing him when he wrote *Henry VIII*. It is implicit in the recurring use of the word 'angel'. The Spanish queen, whose isolation among enemies Shakespeare presents so compassionately, reproaches the English:

> Ye have angels' faces, but heaven knows
> your hearts.[17]

Shakespeare is alluding to the story, which Camden had included in his *Remains*,[18] and which has become part of the national mythology, of St. Gregory's serious joke: a joke itself at once humanitarian and Humanist, at once in love with human beauty and sad at human shortcomings. The line echoes the 'angel' images of *Hamlet* and *Measure for Measure* and implies the whole long debate whether man be angel or beast. There are at least two other 'angel' passages linked with it. The Lord Chancellor, baiting Cranmer, says we are not angels,

> We are all men,
> In our own natures frail, and capable
> Of our own flesh . . .[19]

And Wolsey compares himself with the most spectacular of the angels, Lucifer, and warns Cromwell, warns the audience, against the sin of ambition, which must lead to downfall.[20] *Henry VIII* is a play of tragic falls: the fall of Buckingham, following his father's pattern; the fall of a good Queen; the fall of a Cardinal not good but grand. Critics have said that the play is essentially *De Casibus*. Indeed, it is. But it is not merely a catalogue of falls in the old style, nor does it merely rely on the explanation of 'Fortune's wheel' (that consolation to those who fell, that delusive hope of those who were oppressed and never rose, that *memento mori* and incentive to charity in those who fared well; and that excuse which put events beyond human power and so tended to make men shallower, less self-critical, less reforming). Instead it defines the human context of political crashes; it attributes them to men and explores the process; makes men self-critical. And it adumbrates a theological justification of these falls and the Fall. The tragic *casus* induces what otherwise we would never come to: knowledge of ourselves.

Here Shakespeare's persistent attempt to vindicate human weaknesses intersects with a conviction which he had been developing for some years. The Socratic rule, 'Know thyself', is a Shakespearean touchstone. Perhaps his contemporaries detected its operation in his art; there may be that rare thing in English Renaissance compliments, a genuine sense of parallel, in the second term of the eulogy under the bust in Trinity Church at Stratford-upon-Avon:

Judicio Pylium, genio Socratem, arte Maronem,
    Terra tegit, populus maeret, Olympus habet.[21]
The middle compliment was deserved. Shakespeare with his inquisitive and analytical intellect was the most Socratic of English writers.

It is a commonplace of drama that the characters gain in knowledge as a play evolves. That does not make every dramatist a Socrates. Roxane grows from love of a pretty face to love of a mind, but Rostand is not a Socrates. Shakespeare is not a Socrates in the early plays for though his characters acquire knowledge and even self-knowledge he does not yet employ these terms. *Love's Labour's Lost* would be a good place for their use. The King, Dumain, and Longaville see themselves a little more plainly when, having overheard each other's sonnets, they face their perjury. Biron will know himself better, for knowing the suffering world better, if he survives his twelve months in the hospital. But no. The good medicine is fed without Socratic language to help it down. Richard the Second grows in consciousness from the hour of surrender in Flint Castle through

the scene of deposition and separation from the Queen;
but Shakespeare does not call the process, and the
extremity of pain that accompanies the verbal gymnas-
tics, the conquest of self-knowledge. But by *Measure for
Measure* he is talking about self-knowledge—which was
the Duke's aim 'above all other strifes'.[22] Knowledge
and self-knowledge come to Lear: he has been blind to
the state of his kingdom and its iniquities, and of his
family and its inner oppositions, but when he breaks on
his pride he learns to know them and to know himself.
In the late plays the action rewards the characters with
self-knowledge. Those lines which captivatingly sum
up *The Tempest* tell how

> In one voyage
> Did Claribel her husband find at Tunis,
> And Ferdinand, her brother, found a wife
> Where he himself was lost, Prospero his dukedom
> In a poor isle, and all of us ourselves
> When no man was his own.[23]

In *Henry VIII* the idea is strung across the play. When
the nobles are intriguing against Wolsey, Norfolk says
'The king will know him one day', and Suffolk answers
'Pray God he do! he'll never know himself else'.[24] It's
not clear whether Suffolk means 'Otherwise Wolsey
will never see himself as he is, but will continue to act
the god' or 'Otherwise Henry will never escape from
Wolsey's shadow and see himself as the King with his
duties and powers'. Both results follow from the intrigue. Wolsey falls and:

Cromwell: How does your grace?
Wolsey: Why, well:
> Never so truly happy, my good Cromwell.
> I know myself now.[25]

And Griffith, making his charitable apology for Wolsey, arrives at the same point of repose:

> His overthrow heap'd happiness upon him;
> For then, and not till then, he felt himself . . .[26]

Of course, Wolsey's end is more than repose; it is virtue. In his new tranquillity Wolsey plays the good master: he sends Cromwell to Henry's service and shelter;[27] and this is the sign of virtue, for reciprocal fidelity in master-servant relations, especially if the master falls, is another Shakespearean touchstone. His end is virtue and triumph. It is the justification of Lucifer's fall. Best men are moulded out of faults, alike the faults of their bodies and the more dangerous faults of the head—the faults of the Humanists themselves. They will climb insolently, fall terribly, and come to perfection in the fall.

To translate is to go further than Shakespeare would. But certainly his mind plied these matters as he wrote *Henry VIII*, his interest fully awakened.

What about his interest in the verse?

A decade after Shakespeare's death, Ben Jonson complained that audiences expected the dramatist to gratify the eye. His Prologue to *The Staple of Newes* tells the spectators that their playwrights would rather they came 'to heare, not see a Play':

> Though we his *Actors* must provide for those
> Who are our guests here, in the way of showes,
> The maker hath not so; he'ld have you wise
> Much rather by your eares, then by your eyes.[28]

No doubt we are to take Ben's view of theatrical history with some qualification. For him the stage had never

been wholly what he would have wished it. Even in his
exuberant beginnings the audience had struck him as
inadequately alert to the high and aloof song he fretted.
In later years, when his chair-cracking weight and
pouches frightened the women or made him afraid that
he frightened them, and for disgust of his fat they
undervalued his song, he found in that indignity another focus for his accusation that the judgment of the
eye had superseded the judgment of the ear:

> she hath seene
> My hundreds of gray haires,
> Told seven and fortie yeares,
> Read so much wast, as she cannot imbrace
> My mountaine belly, and my rockie face,
> And all these through her eyes, have stopt her eares.[29]

A lifetime's personal grief against unjust life went into
his thesis of the victorious eye, the failing ear. But had
he not, nevertheless, put his finger on a decisive change
in history? I. A. Richards has pointed out in one of his
most brilliant lectures that the ear of the Elizabethans
and Jacobeans was exquisitely sensitive, tuned by centuries of music, sermons, story-telling; and that our ear
no longer is (but his lecture argues that it might have
been revived by radio, when radio gave us 'the voice
alone', had not television followed too quickly).[30] By its
aural skill an Elizabethan audience could keep up with
actors speaking at torrentially rapid pace, could catch
triple and quadruple puns as they flew past. Now good
drama has, by its nature, always expected to indulge the
eye as well as the ear. Ben Jonson, puristic lover of the
word, was asking too much when he asked the audience
to forgo the rest. Shakespeare, a genuine man of the

theatre, thought in terms of word and action simultaneously, and his rush of words always supposes gestures, looks, movements of muscles and limbs, in
speaker and antagonists. As regards the larger rhythm
of his plays, he always arranged that, while some scenes
should be predominantly idea-studies, *relatively* immobile, the words inviting the mind from the stage to
distant images, other scenes should be immense visual
displays: the 'Russian' masquers in *Love's Labour's
Lost* spring to mind, the Capulet ball in *Romeo and
Juliet*, the Trial scene of *The Merchant of Venice*, Bottom
in his ass's head wooed by Titania and waited on by the
fairies, Richard and Buckingham grotesquely faking
their stand against an imaginary putsch 'in rotten
armour, marvellous ill-favoured'.[31] But to list examples
of the visual corybantics is to see how resourceful
Shakespeare was with a limited range of properties.
Jonson was wrong to allege that good drama had never
needed the eye; but he was right to claim that a change
had occurred: right to remember that suddenly after
1603 much more became available for the eye than the
English stage had ever known; and that once it was
available no one was strong-minded enough to be old-
fashioned and do without. Inigo Jones brought a new
armament of visual effects to Court; he brought it at an
hour when the new Queen, her Danish ear overtaxed
by the profuse language of the playwrights, was demanding less words and more to see and more dancing.
There came those masques in which Ben Jonson and
Inigo Jones collaborated. The lyrics which Jonson
wrote for them are matchless; but evidently the attention, the honours, the highest fees, went to Jones for

the flying gods, the chariots, the fountains and fountain-nymphs, the costumes and engineering. Jonson participated with envy and disgust, in what he thought a process of degeneration.

When a Court inaugurates a fashion, the city hurries after. The public theatres quickly—within three or four years—aped the spectacles of the Court (and started the trend that has turned the theatre from a thrifty to an extravagant and risky financial enterprise). The King's Players were evidently ready enough to go with the stream. From 1607 or 1608 Shakespeare manipulated his scripts to provide opportunites for the engineers and pleasures addressed to the eye. *Pericles* has its storm and its theophany, and its adventures in costume, *Cymbeline* its theophany, *The Winter's Tale* its storm, its sheep-shearing revels, the unveiling of the statue, *The Tempest* a wreck, a magic banquet which appears and disappears, and a masque that is half a theophany. Evidently when *Henry VIII* was contemplated, the company decided that it must be particularly sumptuous, an appeal to the eye more compelling than anything the general public had experienced so far. In performance it was 'set forth', as Sir Henry Wotton's letter describes, 'with many extraordinary circumstances of pomp and majesty, even to the matting of the stage'.[32] Together with processions and pageants, Shakespeare provided, in accordance with his recipe of the period, the half-masque, half-theophany of Katharine's vision.

Henry VIII was a play to delight the eye. But Shakespeare, who agreed with Ben Jonson in so little, did not agree that when the eye was engrossed the ear slept. He saw no reason why. No, not even when the spectacle was lavish. The innovations rather stimulated his verse. It was in the very epoch of engineering and costume that he conducted his dramatic poetry to fresh enterprises.

I will suggest half-a-dozen of his experiments in half-a-dozen telegraphic sentences. He tried his hand at a strongly sculpted poetry for the classical pomp of the theophany in *Cymbeline*. These are strange stanzas;[33] a drama could not support them long; but they are meant as the strange, strong sound of God, and tell of the permanence of heaven as against the uncertainties and fever of man, and depend on their contrast with the staple of the play. The staple is self-interrupting, direction-switching, repetitive phrases of intense speech; and this is a sustained experiment in getting naturalness and humanity from near-incoherence. It is, of course, much stranger and more wonderful than the few stanzas. It is at its most straining and beautiful in the breathless haste of Imogen to be on her way to her husband:

> Then, true Pisanio,—
> Who long'st, like me, to see thy lord; who long'st—
> O, let me bate,—but not like me—yet long'st,
> But in a fainter kind:—O, not like me;
> For mine's beyond beyond—say, and speak thick;
> Love's counsellor should fill the bores of hearing,
> To the smothering of the sense—how far it is
> To this same blessed Milford:[34]

We hear an amazing elaboration of it at the end of the play: Iachimo is making his confession, and the broken phrases register the suffering of a wounded man as well as shame.[35] In the last three plays the broken and re-

petitive phrases, somewhat modified, because the object
now is not to catch the painful joy, the painful haste, the
painful after-experience, of men, but to catch the complexity of the world and man's intense struggle with it,
continue. We hear them in Henry's rebuke to his
Council for misusing 'this good man'.[36] Concurrently,
Shakespeare develops a terse style in which he makes
his impact with a series of nouns:

> . . . holy oil, Edward Confessor's crown,
> The rod, and bird of peace. . . .[37]

or:

> A narrow lane, an old man, and two boys . . .[38]

or:

> . . . did you not name a tempest,
> A birth, and death?[39]

and this is a style which has helped to form the taste of
the present day since Eliot's percipience rediscovered
it and Eliot's skill brought it back into use. And concurrently he takes pleasure in bursts of sensuous, almost
oriental metaphor, as in that line, 'The fringed curtains
of thine eye advance',[40] which Coleridge loved.[41] This
is the obverse of the naked style, just as the obverse of
the speaking style is in that dignified inversion with
which Henry advises Cranmer:

> The best persuasions to the contrary
> Fail not to use, and with what vehemency
> The occasion shall instruct you . . .[42]

There Shakespeare looks forward to Milton. Elsewhere he works for a style of clear pointmaking which
looks forward to the epigram and clarity of those poets
of the next hundred years who, taking the opposite path

to Milton's, aimed at making English as civil a language
as French:

>He gave his honours to the world again,
>His better part to heaven, and slept in peace.[43]

The couplets of *Othello* and *Coriolanus* had tended in
the same direction. It is not too much to say that all the
styles of later English literature can be educed from
Shakespeare's middle and late plays.

But especially from the late plays. You will find there
for example, what you will scarcely find in the middle
plays: the Arcadian rhetoric. 'But that is found in the
early plays! It brims over in *Richard III*!' Yes, so it
does. It *is* used in *Richard III* and swamps some of the
scenes. Shakespeare thought for a spell (in defiance of
the good sense of *Love's Labour's Lost*) that a tragedian
must delight his audiences with the Arcadian artifices.
But because he exploited them most in symmetrical
sequences, in which a line (or a pair of lines, or three
together) spoken by one character, is closely paralleled
in the reply of the next, they led the play from drama
towards opera; and he realized that his theatre stood in
need of greater naturalism, and dropped the sym-
metries and dropped the tropes and worked towards
poetry completely wedded to character and action,
which he established with a first splendid mastery in the
Henry IV sequence. But, absent from the middle plays,
the Arcadian rhetoric is deliberately and delightedly
employed in the late. And now Shakespeare does what
had been beyond his range in the early nineties: uses
the figures Sidney and Spenser adored and uses them
without modulating into opera; uses them without di-
gressing from character; integrates them in the poetry

of action. So the lines about Camillo who tardied the command

> . . . though I with death and with
> Reward did threaten and encourage him,
> Not doing't and being done . . .[44]

and the lines about the shepherd's old, hospitable wife

> . . . her face o'fire
> With labour and the thing she took to quench it.[45]

The non-naturalistic figures are now fused with Shakespeare's naturalism. They do not hold up the drama; they hasten it; make the language not only more energetic but more concise.

All these experiments Shakespeare felt he could the more safely venture when his theatre was gratifying the eye more abundantly.

And he felt free to interpose more scenes in which the characters gather not to act events but to report them. He had, of course, exhibited his pleasure in the poetry of narration before the era of the pageants: he had written Hotspur's speech about the fop on the battlefield, Casca's speech about the offer of the crown to Caesar. I leave it open whether 'The barge she sat in'[46] and Octavius' hardly less brilliant passage about the retreat from Modena[47] preceded the pageant-period or belonged to it. But Shakespeare used his 'reporting' poetry more in the late plays than before, and a great deal in the last of his plays. In *Henry VIII* he included the narratives of the Field of the Cloth of Gold, of Buckingham's trial, of Anne's Coronation, of Wolsey's death.[48] To look at the placing of the last two passages is to see how beautifully Shakespeare developed an art of exchange between the eye and the ear. The voices fall silent and the Coronation procession crosses the stage, magnificent to the eye. Then the voice takes over, the gentleman describing the scene in the Abbey. Immediately follows the scene at Kimbolton, the voice of Griffith narrating Wolsey's last journey. That is immediately followed by the theophany, the masque of the spirits of peace. So the appeal flows from one sense to the other; and Shakespeare incorporates with the new technique his old trick of significant juxtaposition. The new Queen's glory displays the old Queen's poverty, her triumph in Westminster Abbey displays the melancholy of Wolsey's passing in Leicester Abbey, the celestial vision revealed to Katharine displays the impermanence of Anne's triumph. The older he grew, Shakespeare, like all the masters, grew the fonder of 'form', the more susceptible to the pleasure of proving that he could fetter himself and still move freely, as he does in this last play.

Put Away the World-Picture

THIS chapter is the outcome of doubts which have formed and grown over the last ten years: doubts provoked by comments on Shakespeare made, again and again, by students who have been exposed to that teaching of the Elizabethan world-order which I will compendiously call Tillyard's teaching. Before trusting the opinions to type I have looked through the shelf of Tillyard's work; and in his *Muse Unchained*[1] have found so animated an account of the emergence of English studies at Cambridge in this century that I am full of love for him and hardly like to do any of the injuries to his picture that necessity seems to require. But, on reflection, his *Muse Unchained* encourages me. For with that passion for literature, and accordingly for the organically alive, which always impelled him, he shows in his book that academic approaches have their moment of surprise, their hour of energy, and their hour of over-use, mis-use, and decay. That happened, he tells, to the matchless Practical Criticism that Cambridge developed in the twenties. He would have been the first to allow that it must happen to his Order-and-Chain exegesis of the Renaissance mind. I am about to do what he and his Cambridge colleagues would have wished: to indicate the symptoms of over-use and mis-use of his approach.

With each year's efflux from the universities of new teachers trained by Tillyard-directed teachers the order-interpretation of Shakespeare has become the order of the day, and every day has become more formal, more rigid, and less in touch with the feeling of the plays. I will produce one or two examples of undergraduate writing on Shakespeare and suggest that there must be something at fault in a system of teaching which can beget them. Now it may be urged, and is hard to deny, that extraordinary mutilations of *anything* taught will turn up in the writing of undergraduates. But perhaps I shall also be able to quote one or two examples of published criticism by scholars of standing which, however superior the presentation, take the same position that the undergraduates take and perpetrate the same violence.

Shakespeare's art is distinguished from almost any other art of the older writers by its mobility. 'A man knows not where to have him.' He is constantly shifting his position. He moves our sympathies along a route, then about-turns them. Richard II is repugnant, grabbing, earns his overthrow; then is pitiable; then admirable. Caesar is vacillating, pompous, ridiculous; then a sense of his magnanimity and strength streams into the play. We are shifted for and against Hotspur, Hal, Falstaff. Watching Antony we are tugged from position to position, never allowed to settle. Hamlet and Othello are exceptions; perhaps we are with them from start to finish of their plays; all the same, they are shown in varying lights, and we are now drawn closer to them, now half-repelled. Yet this poet whose art is extraordinary by virtue of his power of acrobatic attachment and detachment, his power to see opposites and move between them, whose

> welcome and unwelcome things at once
> 'Tis hard to reconcile,[2]

is now by the fashion of the classrooms tied to a single view of the universe.

Tillyard discovered? composed? the Elizabethan world-picture in the attempt to understand Shakespeare's history-plays. He saw in these plays a description of the violence that sweeps a kingdom, punishing generation on generation, after a capital crime against a king, God's deputy. Now there is not a history-play but shudders with violence and colliding violence. It is true that when the first Tudor wins at Bosworth and unites the houses of York and Lancaster, Shakespeare says that the long sequence of curses has been worked out and order re-established.[3] Tillyard assumed that Shakespeare literally believed in this conclusion. I would rather say that Shakespeare acquiesced in it. I have suggested in another chapter that every Elizabethan knew the sixteenth-century 'order' to be a half-truth. But of course every Elizabethan found it necessary to concur in the Tudor myth. The obligation to salute the régime, this is what Tillyard does not sufficiently allow for. He thinks that Shakespeare elaborated the order-to-disorder, disorder-back-to-order design of the histories from a conviction reached in academic freedom. But it is significant that the one play outside the English histories which unmistakably shows a similar pattern of order-disorder-order is *Macbeth*, another play in which Shakespeare was obliged to remember the feelings of the crown: was writing for James, the titular descendant of Malcolm, and had to pay him the same indirect flattery that he had paid Elizabeth by naming his ancestor the guardian of order. Necessity! The exploitation of necessity was Shakespeare's genius. What he

had to do—for the régime or a patron or the box-office—
he bent into something worth doing. When he had to
represent English history as a tale of crime and re-
peated crime, resolved to harmony at last by Henry
Richmond, he produced an English Oresteia; and when
he had to indulge his Stuart king's preoccupation with
witchcraft and yet represent the Scottish throne as the
seat of order, he produced a furious warring between
cosmic evil and cosmic good. It will be seen that I admit
the presence, or rather some adumbration, of an order
and disorder design in the histories and *Macbeth* and
feel that Tillyard's exposition is here instructive; but
that I think he forgot the conditions which required the
design, grew to over-value it, grew to regard it as the
'net' through which Shakespeare, rendered strangely
immobile and conservative, saw the world. What I most
deplore is the application of the 'net' to plays other than
the histories or *Macbeth*. It has become the habit of Tillyard's school to suppose order as the premise of every
Shakespearean play, to plot an interregnum of disorder
from the second to the penultimate scene, and to hail the
restoration of order in every last scene. This will not do.

It will not do for *King Lear*. Of all Shakespeare's
plays *Lear* is the least susceptible of reduction to ortho-
doxy. It is an attempt by Shakespeare to be bigger than
his time: to see the human predicament afresh. Far
from closing with order restored, it closes in pain and
with its questions unresolved. But before we consider
its close, let us consider its beginning. I read in examin-
ation-papers that there was order in the kingdom and
the mirroring cosmos till Lear broke it by resigning his
crown. Not one word in the play supports this view. On

the contrary, there has been no order under the great
King Lear in the years preceding the action. Shakespeare says so in the sharpest possible way: through
Lear himself: who discovers it when suffering educates
him. In the cold and the storm he learns sympathy for
the first time, and realizes that his kingdom is full of
'wretches' unhoused against the pelting of nature:

> O, I have ta'en
> Too little care of this![4]

and he goes on to recognize the absurdity of a structure
of law upheld by unjust men. Throughout his reign (he
comes to know it) he was a self-willed tyrannical egoist.
A king *is* God's deputy and it is his duty to uphold
God's justice. He witlessly upheld an unjust society.
One of the questions fought out through the sixteenth
century was that of the proper distribution of God's
gifts. It played in Shakespeare's mind, from *The Merchant of Venice* through *Coriolanus*, in its most familiar
form as a question of the distribution of wealth. In
Comus we glimpse Milton interestingly shifting it to
the plane of sex, God's gift of which is inequitably dis-
tributed. Tillyard has no room for it in his world-
picture. Yet in *Lear* it becomes part of the whole fierce
dispute whether savage nature can ever be civilized,
ever be curbed to order.

The trouble thickens as the order-interpreters force
Lear into parallel with the histories. Henry Bolingbroke violated the law of God by deposing a rightful
King and instigating his murder. The order-interpreters
think they must find an equal offence in *Lear*. They can
of course find a very obvious crime in the sub-plot:
Gloucester's adultery in a dark and vicious place. But

in the main plot? They decide that it is as evil for a King to abdicate as for a usurper to depose a King. As Dr. Alice Shalvi, a very capable scholar, puts it in her new book: 'An act of betrayal is ... committed by Lear when, in the play's opening scene, he divests himself of kingship and gives up the divinely-appointed duties of monarchy ... here is the Lord's deputy, divesting himself, most sinfully and criminally, of his divine duty'.[5] This view turns up in undergraduate papers incessantly. It is evidently promulgated in I don't know how many classrooms. But it was unknown to that highly-conscious, highly-religious, sixteenth-century Emperor, Charles V, when he abdicated the sovereignty of the Netherlands in 1555 and of Spain in 1556. Charles' act, says the contemporary chronicler, Gómara, 'causó admiración al mundo par la nouedad y grandeça del negocio'.[6] In English lives of Charles V in the ensuing centuries the step was described as 'heroic'.[7] If Charles and the chronicler had read Tillyard, they might have behaved more decorously; but they had not. Neither had Shakespeare.

Charles and his chronicler and Shakespeare *had* read the Book of Kings, in which David abdicates in favour of Solomon.

I turn from the large plan of *King Lear* to a detail. It is hard to believe that anyone teaches the undergraduate interpretation which follows; but if we do not teach it, we fail to guard against its emergence from what we do teach. When Cornwall's servant opposes the attack on Gloucester's eyes, the students write that he deserves Regan's stab in the back: a man lower in the scale of being has dared to raise his hand against a nobleman.

Again they are pursuing the logic of the argument that condemns Bolingbroke for opposing the King. But the logic is inapplicable. The least attention to Shakespeare's tone would tell a student that. Cornwall's servant says with rough but unmistakable rectitude (he is the moral British yeoman, a thousand years old)

> I have served you ever since I was a child;
> But better service have I never done you
> Than now to bid you hold.[8]

He is as much the good servant as Kent is the good vassal in bidding Lear think again:

> Think'st thou that duty shall have dread to speak
> When power to flattery bows? To plainness
>   honour's bound,
> When majesty stoops to folly.[9]

Can there be any doubt that the one speech and the other are related? The servant is an example of virtue in a bad world. If the Great Men perform the crucial acts in Shakespeare's plays, the common men are very often the Witnesses, sometimes the Judges, occasionally the Shields. The servant does the duty that every great religion requires: he proves his loyalty to his master by trying to prevent him doing wrong (compare the Traditions of Mohammed: '. . . prevent him from doing wrong—that is the definition of loyalty').[10] We may never apply a theory if the application quarrels with the feeling of the play or the poem, nor may we think that an alleged Elizabethan world-picture counts more with Shakespeare than standards that have been pushing forward against brutality across five thousand years. Tillyard, to do him justice, knew this. He supplies, in *Shakespeare's History Plays*,[11] external evidence by

reference to which we can see that Kent and Cornwall's
servant are right. He shows from *A Mirror for Magis-*
trates that 'though loyalty must be carried very far, there
is a point beyond which it must not go' (pp. 85–86) and
from *Woodstock* that 'a man must not obey the king to
the danger of his immortal soul' (p. 119). It follows,
then, that on this particular I am not criticizing Tillyard, who indeed makes strenuous endeavours not to
get lost in his own theory, but those of us who over-
extend his theory.

As for the close of *King Lear*, they are easily appeased
who find that, because Albany and Edgar survive to
sustain the gored state of England, order has been restored in some grander sense: good found strong
enough to resist evil, or God's providence vindicated.
Even Dr. Shalvi, who writes with her hopeful heart that
'A new age is beginning', admits that 'As the curtain
falls, there is a terrible sense of loss'.[12] In *feeling* the last
scene of the play is *tortured*. I use the word deliberately.
For Shakespeare demands it by his image of the rack–
an image as immediate and physical to an Elizabethan
audience as an image of the genital electric shock is to a
modern audience. Lear and Edgar have both counselled
endurance of life from birth to death; but Kent's final
comment, the gleaning of sane experience, is that life is
too terrible for long endurance: let the suffering actor
pass–

> he hates him much
> That would upon the rack of this tough world
> Stretch him out longer.[13]

And *intellectually* the play, far from coming to any point
of equilibrium or rest, ends with the same questioning

that has agitated it throughout. In the course of the action Shakespeare's analytical mind has picked out and held up to the light, examined and offered to us, several possible answers to Lear or Job: that there is an order beneath the cruelty of nature, even a justice, as the blindness of Gloucester and the overthrow of Edmund in the trial by combat show; that there is no order in the cruelty of nature, which hits, with random violence, at those who deserve better, as the death of Cordelia shows; that nature is a confused medley of cruelty and love, and that we must impose a civilizing order on it; that nothing can be done to curb nature, but we must patiently live it; that nothing can be done to curb nature, and that since things cannot 'change' it would be better if things 'ceased'. These tentative answers do not and cannot converge; they diverge and remain divergent; the play ends in intellectual disunity; there is no intellectual reconciliation of the playwright's ideas, no intellectual reconciliation between him and his universe (while, as I have said, the feeling of its ending powerfully condemns the universe). Shakespeare knew that his questioning and some of his answers were unorthodox. Perhaps that is why he speaks of the 'gods' rather than 'God' (and if his 'God' is disguised as 'gods' to circumvent the blasphemy law, I would regard this as another instance where he makes necessity the ally of his meaning). He could more safely venture his unorthodoxy against the 'gods' than against 'God'.

Another play to which the order-teaching cannot be applied, unless with much delicacy, is *Othello*. 'Desdemona', wrote one student in an examination, 'upsets

the natural order of things of the father-daughter relationship by deceiving her father'. Shakespeare, knee-
deep, inch-thick in the father-daughter relationship,
more than once displays that if it is in the natural order
that father and daughter love, it is also in the natural
order that the daughter comes to prefer the husband
and that she will deceive the one to get the other. This
is something that a student is usually well-placed, by
the problem of growing-up, to observe. The examination answer I have quoted shows how much we teachers
have destroyed his native capacity for observation. Even
Bradley did less harm than some of the critical formu-
lae we have taught since 1943; he at least allowed the
flexible play of the student's sense of the common
world. I was once told by a student that order and justice are restored at the end of *Othello*—as at the end of
every Shakespearean tragedy. I asked 'What makes you
think so?' He answered: 'Othello dies and Desdemona
dies'. I asked 'What justice is it that they should die?'
He explained that Desdemona deserved to die for lack-
ing the intelligence to detect Othello's fantasies or the
verbal skill to disarm them; and that Othello deserved
to die for murdering Desdemona and for letting himself
be fooled by Iago. So far will our young people go to
bend a drama to a textbook theory. To any this-world
spectator the success of Iago in destroying Desdemona
and Othello, symbols of the perfect marriage of black
and white, is enough to induce hatred of God. To a pious
spectator it is enough to induce sorrow at the inscruta-
bility of God. A world in which the evil principle can
win such victories is not in any obvious way a world of
justice. Now there may be in fact in the last scene a

gleam of justice or of that regenerating principle of which the critics love to talk: Desdemona's last word.[14] Her last word is a lie, told to save the husband who has strangled her. It drives Othello to the utmost agony; with the simple and ruthless religiosity of a convert he believes her damned for dying with a lie on her lips. We may think that Shakespeare thinks that she is saved by the self-sacrifice of her extreme lie, and that she has won grace for Othello by it: that it is an *imitatio Christi*. But the critics have, as far as I know, let this gleam pass unrecognized; and it may be no gleam; for I have to add, what elsewhere in this chapter I have lodged against the suggestions of other men, that Shakespeare lends not a word to any of the other characters on the stage to bear out the suggestion.

I would rather say of the last scene of *Othello* what I have said of the last scene of *Lear*, and could say of *Hamlet*, that the *feeling*, the *mood*, is not that of order restored nor of redemption won. There are later works, notably *Cymbeline*, which laud the gods at their close. But the tragedies end in horror at the evil of life. 'In this harsh world draw thy breath in pain.'[15] They are as uncompromisingly sombre as Euripides' 'If we are still to live after this life I don't know what remedy there is for the pain of mortals'.[16] At the very least this must be said of the Shakespeare of the tragedies: that there were times when he thought, felt, and dramatized attitudes which owe nothing to the 'world-picture'; and, what is distinctly to the point, that these attitudes sometimes energize his highest work.

If, in affection for the Tillyard of the unchaining, and in the faith that he was sensitive to the limitations of the

chain-of-being, I have seemed to exculpate him entirely from the faults of his flock, let me now add that
his own arguing, for all its bulk of evidence on the one
side and its refinement on the other, has its blind-spots.
He leaned heavily on Ulysses' speech on degree and on
Davies' *Orchestra*. He asks us to weigh these well, almost to accept them as the Elizabethan testament. They
are wonderful, and we have to be grateful for any direction that sends us to them. But that they are positive
statements of the thinking of the time is not to be
assumed without pause. To each of them there is a
peculiarly negative aspect. One thing we are certain of
about *Troilus and Cressida* is that the British audience
identified with the Trojans. We are also certain of the
predominant tone of the play, by which both sides are
blamed: idiots both, to spill blood for a trollop. It is also
clear that as between the two sides the Trojans represent a more agreeable kind of man, debonair, in-
clined to honour, as compared with the Greeks, who
are either witless muscle or tricky exploitatory craft.
Ulysses may be the cleverest man on the stage, but it is
by no means certain that Shakespeare meant the spectators to like him. It is probable that Shakespeare was
deliberately executing the same surprising inversion of
a classical reputation that he elsewhere executed with
Caesar and, for a brief flash, with Cicero.[17] Whereas
Troy faintly adumbrates an ideal of human freedom, a
society in which, free to be fair or unfair, the best men
will try to be fair, the Greeks decisively look towards an
ideal of a State welded into 'order', cohesion, a battering-ram. Ulysses wants degree to be observed because
he wants the battering-ram to function and crush

feckless and dainty Troy (lightly-sketched symbol of an England which Shakespeare liked and thought doomed). Ulysses and the Cabinet of schemers manipulate the capricious letter-men of their team till the wedge is solid. These considerations make it very difficult to receive the speech on degree as an image of something Shakespeare approves.

If the degree speech is indeed the summation of a familiar Elizabethan concept of order, its adoption by Ulysses, its appropriacy to the Greeks, show that Shakespeare was capable of an extraordinary detachment from it. He may have foreseen—if Hotson is right in guessing that *Troilus* was written for the Middle Temple[18]—that the greybeards, long-arrived judges, in his first-night audience would wag their beards sagely as Ulysses went through the steps of the speech, approving the doctrine that upheld the status quo. But by the same token he must have known that it would sound fusty to the questioning young wits of his audience, the Donnes, the roistering up-and-comingers: as fusty and as hateful as it sounded to the rebel side, or the Falstaffian side, of his own split personality. Tillyard knew that Donne was no invariable subscriber to his world-picture, and reacted by suggesting that Donne was *therefore* not quite so good a poet as twentieth-century fashion thinks. But the Donnes of the nineties formed, and it does not matter whether in the Middle Temple, as Hotson suggests, or in a more public arena, a part of the audience for which Shakespeare wrote—and a part whose critical acumen he probably recognized.

Of course, it is the excellence of the poetry that convinces Tillyard that he can use the degree speech as a prop of his case. Yet Tillyard himself very beautifully said, dealing with a different play, that good poetry in Shakespeare is not a sign of the dramatist's *approval* but of his *interest* in the character's argument. Some of the best poetry in Shakespeare is written for Caliban.

What Tillyard does not tell us, but it is relevant to any discussion of Ulysses, is that Shakespeare gradually developed certain personal opinions so strong that they burst out of the framework of the individual drama and assert themselves across the corpus of his work, and that one such opinion is that politicians are anti-human. Brutus is a non-politician accepting the responsibility of politics, and in the outcome suffering consequences that make us despair: as far as he learns political practice he is bloodied; as far as his humanity remains intact he bungles; by his very decency he fails. Those who know the ropes and pull them expertly are indecent. Terrible the managers of men. Ulysses is one of these, the most adroit and therefore the most dangerous.

A little more may be said about the politicians while we are with them. Taste and honesty lead Tillyard from time to time to clarify aspects of Shakespeare which are outside the order-disorder concept. So he very finely—not all-inclusively, but finely as far as he goes—discusses the psychological authenticity of the father-son trouble between the King and Hal. But at one point where a keen analysis of a political sequence in *Henry IV* would lead him into a difficulty with the order-disorder thesis he can be caught crying off. You will find in his *History Plays* no careful account of the events in Gaultree Forest. Yet in a structure as brilliantly cohesive as that

of the *Henry IV* double, these events must be important.
The sequence which studies Prince John at Gaultree is
the equivalent and counter-balance of the sequence
which studies Worcester at Shrewsbury, and is equally
damning to both politicians. Cold Lancaster inherits
his father's treacherous statecraft. Tillyard's discrimina-
tion tells him that Shakespeare intended to condemn
Lancaster; and he writes a sentence: 'The justice of
John of Lancaster in his cold-blooded treatment of the
rebels verges on rigour' (p. 266).[19] But that is a pulled
punch; and it is tucked away in a paragraph about other
affairs; and Tillyard moves quickly on. Any full examination of the 'justice' of the case must have dented the
world-picture. The royal forces (the forces of 'order'!)
stand convicted in those two hard scenes; and to the
rebel leaders there accretes, as there always must to
those who are shockingly cheated, shockingly put to
death, an aura of martyrdom. Hardin Craig has a foot-
note to his text of the play asking us to understand the
scenes in the light of the world-picture: 'Prince John's
perfidy seems nowhere to be censured by Shakespeare;
this possibly finds its explanation in the theory of the
time with regard to rebels'.[20] But the whole tone of the
sequence is a censure. And the action is a censure: for it
is a tradition that, when you have drunk with a man,
even your enemy, you may do him no harm. The world-
picture has led our scholars and students to slide over
material that will not fit, to shut their ears to Shakespeare's tone, to preserve their theories in defiance of
the plays.

Tillyard, borrowing, with acknowledgments, from
Hart, conjectures that Shakespeare never forgot the

sermons against rebellion that he heard in boyhood as
the royalist troops marched north to put down the rising of 1569.[21] Maybe not. But as words held in a man's
memory since childhood come back to him in age he is
apt to reflect on them with wonder and curiosity and
see them in an entirely new light, and answers rise
against them. He sees the other side, the more because
in boyhood he could not see it. Where Hart and Tillyard use the boyhood experience to prove that Shakespeare endorsed the world-picture, I would rather use
it to explain how he became capable of questioning
the world-picture and dramatizing the 'rigour' of the
powers-that-be and the viewpoint of the insurgents and
the suppressed. I do not want to rush from Tillyard's
doctrine to the opposite extreme. It certainly seemed
better to Shakespeare to live in the relative peace of his
time than in the fifteenth century when family was
divided against family. He filled out more and more
into the successful man of property, who depends on
tranquillity and 'order'. But the inquisitive poet in him
survived the process, and drew both on the process and
on the psychic counter-trends success creates; drew too
on the different experience of the lost and early London
years when he was in outer darkness, still had all to
prove, and might identify with the unlanded younger
sons and shout like Falstaff 'they hate us youth'.[22] His
plays censure the mob, fear lawlessness, praise the
sturdy soundness of Iden or the shrewdness of Lafeu.
But there are moments when he makes beautiful the
thrust for change, which history calls rebellion and
Tillyard disorder. The conspirators in Rome were
'courtiers of beauteous freedom'.[23] Hotspur, Glen-

dower, and Mortimer (though not the political Worcester who eggs them on) are courtiers of beauty, though a beauty which, entrancedly pursuing her, they do not understand—so much becomes marvellously clear to anyone who, at a good performance, has sat breathless while the conspirators listen to the haunting Welsh song in Bangor Castle.[24]

Everything in Shakespeare becomes clear provided that we listen. Tillyard sometimes closed his ear, annulled his genuine care for poetry. He was determined to do down *Henry V*, because it jarred against his theory and because he fastidiously recoiled from the rather loud patriotism he thought it professed. He skimmed over it rapidly. He would not let himself enjoy the Eve of Agincourt: 'Henry's conversation with Bates and Williams . . . has the chill of Brutus's speech over Caesar's body rather than the warmth of the prose of the previous plays'.[25] This is a tone-deaf judgment, a judgment which the searching voices of Olivier's film, wonderful in these minutes, declare untenable. If Tillyard had listened to them his honesty must have made him report and reflect on the spirit of questioning abroad in the age and at its most alert in Shakespeare. And I do not know how Hardin Craig, with a scene like this standing against him, holds that Shakespeare's century neither practised nor valued questioning.

And what about *Orchestra*? If we must be cautious about Ulysses' speech, we must be equally cautious here. *Orchestra* is a lovely poem; but not a central poem; and not an unambiguous poem. The significance of Penelope, for the Elizabethans as for Homer and for everyone until Joyce, was her fidelity—her resistance to the suitors despite the dancing figures and the tidal changes of the womb. Now *Orchestra* is the coruscation of amorous enthusiasm. Davies imagines and executes it as a young man to whom the seduction of women is naturally exciting, and the breaking of marriages desirable; for to a young man marriage is an image of the old order which he thinks of as a hedge of spears against his merit, and which he must rupture, he must. If the charming Antinous has his way and Penelope steps out of her seclusion into the dance, it will be the end of fidelity. In fact this poem, which Tillyard claims to be a projection of the Elizabethan sense of the order that runs through and relates all constitutions and undertakings, and which in its episodes and *exempla* is indeed so designed and so functions, has a plot which, if pushed to its climax, must spell a breach of the holy order of marriage. The poem is unfinished. And I fancy that it is unfinished because Davies saw the contradiction. It was irreconcilable, and he could not let the music go further. Enthusiasm faltered, passion cooled, and he left a beautiful fragment which sets the Word against the Word: young man's world-picture athwart old man's world-picture; world-picture of the have-nots against world-picture of the haves.

So, if I am in any measure right, the two main supports of Tillyard's structure are queer supports. And some of his flourishes are queer. He says, with pleasure in the discovery, that Milton, who once seemed an individual apart, was a Renaissance man and wrote in terms of the world-picture. This is true, but makes the famous paradoxes of his epic more glaring. Just as the vicious Ulysses is the spokesman of degree, the subversive Satan is a spokesman of the heavenly hierarchy: 'Not to know mee argues your selves unknown'.[26] And Milton, champion of God and poet of a fabric of order in which regicide is a symbolic attack on God, was one of the regicides.

It has been a good discipline for scholars of literature to examine Elizabethan documents of many kinds and to educe and codify the lore that we have come to call the world-picture. But we must know where the world-picture can help us to understand the great literature better and where it may be of less help than general literary sensibility. I am not trying to drive it into limbo. As Tillyard and Hardin Craig have often shown, to our profit, there are passages in Shakespeare—like Lorenzo's exposition of the immortal harmony[27]—that can best be understood beside the picture of former heaven. The world-picture is an indispensable instrument for explaining allusions such as this. But we must not think that because Shakespeare was an Elizabethan he was not a man, and we must not suppose that men then were very different than they are now. It may be constricting rather than educative to read him, as Dover Wilson once implied we should, 'with Elizabethan spectacles'.

Anyone who over-stresses the importance of the world-picture in any age makes two mistakes. First, he assumes that men only think in one set of terms. This is not the case. Men hold a number of beliefs, discrepant and mutually exclusive, in the same age and at the same moment; they hold and use concurrently old beliefs, new beliefs, and intimations of beliefs of unborn epochs. Secondly, he assumes that men are so responsive to their environment, so mobile in mind and quick to

change, that because we shoot the moon and film-stars
we now think differently than Shakespeare even on all
those common problems that have not altered since the
Pharaohs. 'Man is changed by his living; but not fast
enough', says Auden:[28] 'In the hour of the Blue Bird
and the Bristol Bomber, his thoughts are appropriate to
the years of the Penny Farthing'. Auden might be more
severe. Our thoughts are very often appropriate to the
years of the roan or the foot-traveller's staff. Every
Englishman still has Shakespeare's Englishmen alive in
his bones and brains: can practically feel their presence,
their habits and tics; they are only twelve grandfathers
back. The words are nearly the same, the tones are
utterly the same. When Shakespeare wishes a character
to be most completely sincere—when Hamlet talks to
Horatio, for example—he uses the same English that
we use in our best intimacy.[29] When a character is re-
signedly, sceptically, yet not hostilely, dry, like the
King in *All's Well* turning aside flattery: 'I fill a place,
I know 't':[30] the tone is as completely modern as
Elizabethan. We are in direct touch with Shakespeare.
It is not, as Jan Kott nicely urged, that he is our contemporary, but that we are still his. The sun-stars-and-
earth picture has changed, but the business and problems of living have not changed, and our capacity for
living alone has not improved, still less our capacity for
living in society. I doubt whether Elizabethan man
made any different use of his astronomical, and the
inter-connected ethical, picture than we do of ours.
They and we get occasional help, occasional admonition, occasional restraint from some phrase, some image
dependent on the contemporary picture. But they and

we do not live in accordance with the picture. In fact, comparing us to the Elizabethans, I am scarcely severer than Auden. We have to be much harsher. Man's mind is still near the beginning of things. The Elizabethans lived, and we live, pre-historic patterns of behaviour: behaviour of the caves, the forests, the stone circles, the mating arena. Shakespeare was living these patterns, as was pomaded Ovid and disputing Plato. Man has been changed by his living, but only at the top of his head. At the top of his head, addressing his living but not much heard, sometimes modifying it a little, but not much, are the various attitudes to the universe that he entertains and entertains simultaneously.

It is an aid to a man or a nation to invent an image of perfection and to keep it alive through the weathers of bloodymindedness and profit. The Renaissance hierarchies were, I hasten to concede to Tillyard, a civilizing influence at the top of the head. They did something to Shakespeare and the Shakespearean audience. But they were not the only such influence. Nor the chief. Obviously a stronger influence was the Bible. Tillyard made a perfunctory bow to the Bible, but did not care to think about it much, because 'Shakespeare and the Bible' was old hat. And because the text was often inconvenient. The scripture can, of course, be cited by all parties, and he winkled out and cited a verse precisely to his taste:

> Let every soul submit himself unto the authority of the higher powers: for there is no power but of God: the powers that be, be ordered of God. Whosoever therefore resisteth the power, resisteth the ordinance of God: but they that resist shall receive to themselves damnation.[31]

185

—one of the Pauline texts that comfort the conservatives.
But England's appeal to the Bible has never been predominantly conservative. Moreover, the sixteenth century was the age of the Bible recaptured for the laity,
and the Bible recaptured for the laity was also the Bible
re-read for the underdog. If the pressure of the doctrine
of the hierarchies tended to discourage rebellion, tended to discourage even questioning, the Bible in the
vernacular tended to encourage questioning, certainly,
and even rebellion. The militancy of the prophets who
harangued kings, the rebukes of Christ, the patience of
Christ, the distributism of Christ's mission to the poor,
are patterns—which the order-theory cannot provide—
for the oscillations of the Christianized saga-prince,
Hamlet, the heart-searching of outcast Lear. And we
know other patterns of thought affecting the writers
and the audience: Copernicus, Machiavelli, Cicero,
Aristotle. These mixed pulls and counter-pulls worked
just as much and just as little as the hierarchies on the
thought of Shakespeare and the audience; and just as
much and just as little inform the plays.

Tillyard wished on Shakespeare his own passion for
order. He expounded the World-Picture as his society
disintegrated into the Second World War, as it fought
the War and remade itself and came out different. In
anger at the wrongs done in the Europe of the thirties,
he welcomed the army of unalterable law and chained
Falstaff. He allows us to like the Boar's Head Tavern
so long as we never go. The celerity with which the
Picture was adopted suggests that one wing of the
Academy of our time has shared his apprehension of
lawlessness, his love of respectability.

There are, however, among the scholars who teach on Tillyard lines many for whom the merely respectable is anathema, but who succumb to a nobler temptation: a longing to improve the world; a sense that evil forces are very strong, a passion to enlist against them. Dr. Shalvi, whom I invoke again for her excellence and because she is, if I am not mistaken, a graduate of the Cambridge of the forties, writes of *Macbeth* and its 'restorative message':

> As in *King Lear* what we see here is a man doing his best to destroy the divinely-created perfection of the ordered universe of which he is an integral part. And, as in the earlier play, we see other men, suffering, selfless, and heroic, opposing the forces of evil and ultimately triumphing over them. The Sons of Light overthrow the Sons of Darkness.[33]

The last sentence is the triumph of Salvationism and Uplift. This is not a deadly sin. The danger is that it may be illusion. We may choose to hope not. However, the peculiar fact I am anxious to pin is that many critics whose drive is towards uplift, which is a process of world-changing, are mysteriously caught in the Tillyard pattern of order, which is a doctrine of resistance to change. It would be well for every critic and every teacher to decide what he really wants. And then to excuse Shakespeare from complicity.

* * *

For these reasons I move for a moratorium on the teaching of the order-theory as the decisive background of Shakespeare. As long as the order-theory prevails we can hardly admit that, stalking cautiously and delicately between the traps of his time and of his vices, he is an explorer. But he is.

Will any teacher be left at a loss if the order-theory is dropped? I doubt it. Every teacher in school or university uses several approaches to the plays in tandem. But let me suppose, improbably, that someone has been teaching Shakespeare by the sole support of the Picture for twenty years, and now asks what he can use instead. There are at least four good approaches. The first, of proved reliability, is that which Nevill Coghill demonstrates in *Shakespeare's Professional Skills*: the reconstruction of Shakespeare's difficulties and opportunities as the player-actor, the man working with a stock company and writing to get the best out of his fellow-actors, whose capabilities he knows from experience; to get the best out of the props commonly available; to give the crowd the tricks it expects and to surprise it by more than it expects.[33] Much detail in the plays becomes alive under this analysis. And then the total effect of the play may become clearer for the greater clarity of the detail. That ear-splitting moment in the fourth act of *Richard III*, for example, when Richard orders his drums and trumpets to drown the shrieking women:[34] the air is in tumult; absurd tumult; and we recognize the comedy of noise as one of the methods of this atrociously comic tragedy; and then the more sharply understand the tragic restlessness of Richard; he never sleeps; he never lets his wife or his assassins sleep; as elsewhere in Shakespeare energy has turned into its lethal negative. And the 'professional' approach is not only a matter of the recovery of Tudor and Jacobean conditions. It includes the study of performances of Shakespeare at all times, including the present: what have directors and actors tried to do? how far have they succeeded? what light has their interpretation thrown on a play? A second approach, much worked but still fruitful, is the examination of Shakespeare's style, and especially of the changes in his style over the course of his career. There is, for example, something to be conjectured about Shakespeare's shorthand poetry: the packed phrase, like 'Our lives' sweetness':[35] phrases in which a view of life is concentrated as if there were only a moment to squeeze it into the dialogue amid so much to be done, so much to be written. If *Lear* and *Othello* are written at much the same period of Shakespeare's life, why are the shorthand phrases found in *Lear* rather than *Othello*? And why is it that the last scene of *Lear* is stylistically so close to the last scene of *Antony and Cleopatra*—its elevation and intensity produced by short broken-off phrases, gasps, interjections exchanged between characters like powerful musical phrases? There is a great difference in the demand the two scenes make on us, and in the coloration with which they make it: *Lear* appals us by the hardly-respired bizarre gasps of men looking at doomsday, drives us to hate events and appetites that can so end; *Antony* provokes us to concurrence in the life that can end in the ecstasy of death by orgasm. Different the tonality; yet both scenes work through the same peculiarly Shakespearean development, the rhetoric of the broken phrase. A third approach is the investigation of the geology of the images of the sixteenth and seventeenth centuries. The most massive images of a work of literature may occasionally be the product of the individual psychology of the writer and may stand separate from his age. But often they jut from a submerged reef of common experience, often they are evidence of material in convulsion below the crust of civilization. Much can be learned by plotting the minor versions that precede the enormous versions of an image. Think of the allusions to Orpheus, among them the song in *Henry VIII*,[36] in the poets preceding Milton, and how Milton then makes Orpheus one of his vital personae: hurls up the lines in *Lycidas*,[37] in effect calling himself an Orpheus, and proving himself an Orpheus by the fierce river-music, and predicting that mad women, who are sexuality on the rampage, will destroy him like Orpheus. And Milton goes on seething with the material, which breaks out again and spills in mountainous Rhodope

> where Woods and Rocks had Eares
> To rapture, till the savage clamor dround
> Both Harp and Voice; nor could the Muse defend
> Her Son.[38]

Milton is able to raise the common image to sublimity because the conception of the primal poet, torn to pieces by stimulated women, directly touches his desire for and decapitating fear of carnal frenzy. How the personal sensibility fuses with the imagery common to an age we can see at this point. We can learn much by the accumulation of examples of other images in the late Renaissance poets, and especially in Shakespeare; and what awaits enquiry is the process by which the collective imagery is formed and gathers and asserts its historical meaning. For a fourth approach let us do what has often been done and read Shakespeare in the light of our own problems, our own conduct and misconduct, still so near to and so like his own. Here I may seem to forget my own warning against making Shakespeare an accom-

plice. But not so. The work I propose will be done with
a great deal of personal consciousness; it will be a truly
critical process: that is, we have both to respond to
Shakespeare and to watch ourselves responding, we
have both to identify with him and to hold ourselves
separate and watch and correct the process of identification. Tillyard did not read Shakespeare in the light of
his private problems, but in the dark of his private problems; he identified without always knowing that he
identified, and then he limited Shakespeare, expected
Shakespeare to think as he thought. We must not con-
fuse a writer's events or his commentary with what we
hope. But we may understand him by what we *know*.
Going to meet him with what we know, including what
we know of our habits of forgetting our habits, what we
know of our tendency to make him merely reflect our
hopes and fears, we may understand him and then
understand ourselves better, since he sees further into
human processes and with more subtlety. We can begin with a phrase. There comes a phrase—'Forgive me
this my virtue'[39]—that makes us pause by its ring of
introspection and its knowledge of the self, and that yet
implies a knowledge of others, of the family and its collisions, of society and its collisions; we can begin there
and work inward and outward along the patterns Shakespeare draws through a drama. Scholars are sometimes
shy of this procedure, drive their colleagues off it by
labelling it 'impressionism'. But if this is impressionism,
let critics practise it. It is a function by which the self,
in play with a work of art, changes, however imper-
ceptibly, and because it changes changes the world.

Notes

CHAPTER I

1. *Jonsonus Virbius*, 1638. Easily accessible in Jonson, *Works*, ed. Herford and Simpson, Vol. XI (Oxford, Clarendon Press, 1952), 428 ff.
2. Anonymous. Published by T. Marshe in 1555 and again in 1568. (S.T.C. 14104 and 14105.)
3. *I, William Shakespeare* (New York, O.U.P., 1938) 142.
4. *King John* III i 326 ff.
5. *King John* IV i 41 ff.
6. Meres, *Palladis Tamia*, 1598: 'so the sweet witty soul of Ovid lives in the mellifluous and honey-tongued Shakespeare'.
7. *Venus and Adonis* 872–3.
8. *Two Gentlemen* I iii 31.
9. *Venus and Adonis* 1177–86.
10. As promised in the Dedication of *Venus and Adonis*: 'if your honour seem but pleased I account myself highly praised, and vow to take advantage of all idle hours, till I have honoured you with some graver labour'.
11. See E. K. Chambers, *William Shakespeare* (Oxford, Clarendon Press, 1930) Vol. II, 18–32.
12. See e.g. G. B. Harrison, *The Life and Death of Robert Devereux, Earl of Essex* (London, Cassell, 1937) 111–21.
13. *Midsummer Night's Dream* II i 67.
14. See J. A. K. Thomson, *Shakespeare and the Classics* (London, Allen and Unwin, 1952) 77.
15. *Midsummer Night's Dream* II i 107–11.
16. This remark is, admittedly, debatable. Ezra Pound has said that Tudor Englishmen were 'Latin'–i.e. they lent themselves to an unrestrained 'acting-in-life', a display of all the emotions. There is an element of truth in that, if we contrast Shakespearean customs with the late nineteenth-century English etiquette of the stiff upper lip. But Sidney's demeanour shows, I think, that the doctrine of restraint either held in Court or was coming into Court by 1570; and between 1590 and 1600 Shakespeare teaches it as the definitive style of the gentleman. So, for example, Hamlet's modesty: 'I shall win at the odds', which does not claim the ability to win outright (when the duel begins we see that he *can* win outright, but he would not, even in a private murmur to his best friend, be brash and

exhibitionist enough to say so); he only claims the ability to prevent Laertes finishing more than two hits ahead.

17. *The Merchant* III ii 223 ff.
18. *The Merchant* III ii 258 ff.
19. '*The Courtier* was one of the key-books of the English Renaissance. Hoby's translation, first printed in 1561, passed through new editions in 1577, 1588, and 1603. And to realize how seriously the book was read it is necessary only to know that a Latin translation by Bartholomew Clarke, issued in 1571, achieved an even greater popularity than Hoby's work, reaching its sixth edition by 1612.' (F. O. Matthiessen, *Translation: an Elizabethan Art* (reprinted New York, Octagon Books, 1965) 12.
20. '. . . I haue found in diuers smally learned Courtiers a more sounde stile than in some professors of learning . . .' *An Apology for Poetry,* in, e.g., G. Gregory Smith, *Elizabethan Critical Essays,* Vol. I (London, O.U.P., 1904) 203.
21. *Much Ado* II i 334 ff.
22. In his *Complete Works of Shakespeare* (Chicago, Scott, Foresman, 1951) 531–2.
23. *Much Ado* IV i 305 ff.
24. *Hamlet* III i 125.
25. *Troilus and Cressida* I ii 6.
26. *Troilus and Cressida* V iii 1–2.
27. *All's Well* II iii 208.
28. *Coriolanus* II i 26.
29. *Coriolanus* III i 72.
30. *Coriolanus* I ix 79–91.
31. *Coriolanus* I iv 58–61.
32. *Coriolanus* I v 25–7.
33. *Coriolanus* I iii 71.
34. *As You Like It* I vii 118.
35. *Coriolanus* V iii 188.
36. *Coriolanus* V v 4–5.
37. *Tempest* I ii 120.
38. *Henry VIII* V v 37–9.
39. *Winter's Tale* IV iv 92 ff.
40. *Pericles* V i 96.
41. *Cymbeline* V v 229.
42. *Winter's Tale* I ii 391–3.
43. *Hamlet* III ii 1–16.

CHAPTER II

1. Quoted in Joan Grundy, *The Poems of Henry Constable* (Liverpool, 1960) 35.
2. In 'Colin Clout's Come Home Againe' 377–9.
3. See John Dickenson, *Arisbas* (London, Thomas Creede for Thomas Woodcocke, 1594). In his address 'To the Gentlemen-Readers' Dickenson laments Sidney's death: '. . . the whitest Swanne and sweetest of APOLLOES musicall birdes, hath put an endlesse periode to his ever-living lines. . . .'
4. See Sidney, *An Apology for Poetry*, in e.g. G. Gregory Smith, *Elizabethan Critical Essays* Vol. I (London, O.U.P., 1904) 179.
5. See Gabriel Harvey's letter in e.g. G. Gregory Smith, Vol. I, 89.
6. In his *Mr. W. H.* (London, 1964) 195–7.
7. 1 *Henry VI* I iv 70; IV iii–iv; IV v–vii.
8. 1 *Henry VI* I ii 130–5; I iv 35; III ii 104–5; IV i 9–47.
9. 2 *Henry VI* III ii 153–7
10. 3 *Henry VI* iii 6–52.
11. 2 *Henry VI* IV viii 36 ff.
12. Cf. Nevill Coghill's comments in *Shakespeare's Professional Skills* (Cambridge, C.U.P., 1964) 206.
13. In his *William Shakespeare: the Complete Works* (New York, Harper and Brothers, n.d.) 549.
14. In 1 *Henry VI* II v and 1 *Henry IV* I iii 145 ff.
15. *Henry V* IV i 11–17.
16. *Henry V* IV i 102 ff.
17. *Henry V* II iii 59.
18. *Henry V* IV i 311.
19. *Richard II* II i 40 ff.
20. 2 *Henry VI* IV x 21–5.
21. *Richard III* III vi.
22. *Richard II* III ii 24 ff.
23. e.g. 1 *Henry IV* I i 26–8 and *Measure for Measure* II ii 73–5.
24. *Dr. Faustus* V ii 150.
25. See e.g. Lucy Aiken, *Memoirs of the Court of James I* (Boston, 1822) Vol. I, 85; William McElwee, *The Wisest Fool in Christendom* (London, Faber, 1958) 111.
26. McElwee 121–2.
27. In *Renaissance News* Vol. XVIII, No. 2 (Summer 1965) 179.
28. 2 *Henry VI* IV i 92–117.
29. 2 *Henry VI* IV vii 30 ff., e.g. 'Thou hast most traitorously corrupted the youth of the realm in erecting a grammer school . . .'
30. *Julius Caesar* III iii.

NOTES

CHAPTER III

1. For the details in this paragraph see H. H. Furness, *A New Variorum Edition of Shakespeare: The Merchant of Venice* (first published 1888, reissued New York, American Scholar Publications, 1965) 395–9. J. R. Brown in the Arden Edition of the play (London, 1955) gives a valuable, succinct survey of the Lopez material but does not set great store by it as an explanation of the play – or of any passage.
2. In *Il Pecorone*. See Furness *op. cit.*, Brown *op. cit.*, and G. Bullough, *Narrative and Dramatic Sources of Shakespeare* Vol. I (London, Routledge and Kegan Paul, 1957) 449, 463–76.
3. I.e. Job. The name 'Gobbo', drawn from Q2, is usually adopted. But 'Iobbe' appears in Q1 and F; it is rendered as 'Job' in F3; and evidently Shakespeare intended this great name, coupled absurdly with the name of Launcelot.
4. Cf. George Unwin in *Shakespeare's England* (Oxford, Clarendon Press, 1916) Vol. I, 332. See also Henry S. Swabey, 'The English Church and Money', *The Criterion*, July, 1937.
5. *The Merchant* I i 163.
6. *The Merchant* III iv 3.
7. 122–3.
8. *The Merchant* I i 50–5.
9. *Much Ado* III i 6–11.
10. *The Merchant* III ii 297–9.
11. *The Merchant* II i 264 cf. IV i 11.
12. *The Merchant* I iii 129–32.
13. *The Merchant* I iii 133–8.
14. See especially Nevill Coghill, *Shakespeare Quarterly* I (London, 1948) 9–17.
15. *The Merchant* I ii 15 ff.
16. In this allusion to 'slaves' it is tempting to see a clue to an undetected source of the play, a work in which the scene is set in a region Turkish, Arabic, or African, accustomed to slavery. But if Shakespeare used such a source, what is most interesting is his recollection of the slaves at a moment when he needs material for Christian self-criticism; he is prepared to transfer the practice of slavery to the Venetians for the sake of this result.
17. *The Merchant* III i 54–76.
18. Cf. a curious sentence in Burke's *Reflections on the Revolution in France*. The spine of the sentence is: 'The men of England . . . would be ashamed, as of a silly, deceitful trick, to profess any religion in name, which by their proceedings they appear to contemn.' The complete sentence is heavily qualified: 'The men of

England, the men, I mean, of light and leading in England, whose wisdom (if they have any) is open and direct, would be ashamed, as of a silly, deceitful trick, to profess any religion in name, which, by their proceedings, they appear to contemn'. (*Works of Edmund Burke*, Vol. III (Boston, Little, Browne, 1884) 365.

19. See H. H. Furness, *op. cit.*, ix, x, xi.
20. *The Merchant* I iii 78 ff.
21. *The Merchant* III v 74, cf. *Twelfth Night* III i 13.
22. *The Merchant* V i 91.
23. *Shakespeare and the Tragic Pattern, Proc. of the Brit. Acad. 1958* (London, 1959) 154.
24. *Hamlet* I i 166.
25. *Hamlet* I v 92–5.
26. *Hamlet* IV v 131–3.
27. *Hamlet* II ii 599–604.
28. *Hamlet* IV iv 38.
29. *Hamlet* IV v 86.
30. *Hamlet* IV iv 56–9.
31. III iii and III iv.
32. *Hamlet* II ii 258 ff.
33. *Hamlet* V ii 7.
34. In his *John Lyly* (London, Routledge, 1962) 51.
35. In *The Sacred Wood* (London, Methuen, 1920) 92–3.
36. *Love's Labour's Lost* I i 3.

CHAPTER IV

1. Edward Arber, *A Transcript of the Register of the Company of Stationers of London* Vol. III (London, 1876) 316 and 316 b.
2. *Shakespeare's Satire* (London, O.U.P., 1943).
3. *Hamlet* II ii 354–78.
4. *Antony and Cleopatra* III xiii 43–6.
5. Audrey calls him an 'old gentleman' (V i 4). Am I taking her too seriously? Perhaps the point is that Jacques is not a very old gentleman and would have been furious at the description.
6. *As You Like It* IV i 5–7.
7. *As You Like It* III ii 298–9.
8. *As You Like It* I ii 90 ff.
9. *The Shepheardes Complaint. A passionate Eclogue, written in English Hexameter,* in which the poet is 'transported into the blessed soile of heavenly *Arcadia*' (London, [E. Allde] for William Blackewall, n.d. [S.T.C. says 1596]).
10. *Chloris, or the complaint of the passionate despised Shepheard*

(London, Edm. Bollifant, 1596). Smith's dedication is addressed 'TO THE MOST EXCELLENT / and learned Shepheard / Collin Cloute'.

11. See e.g. G. Bullough, *Narrative and Dramatic Sources of Shakespeare* Vol. II (London, Routledge, 1958) 143–256.

12. Drayton, *Polyolbion*, 'The Thirteenth Song', 35–8. See e.g. Drayton, *Poems* ed. John Buxton (London, Routledge, 1953) Vol. II, 587.

13. Dekker, *Patient Grissil*, ed. J. P. Collier (London, Shakespeare Society, 1841) 8–9.

14. *As You Like It* II v 20 ff. and III ii 317 ff.

15. *As You Like It* I ii 34–57.

16. *As You Like It* V iv 165–71.

17. *As You Like It* I iii 77.

18. *As You Like It* V iv 113 ff.

19. Arber, *loc. cit.*

20. *As You Like It* III v 82.

21. *As You Like It* III iii 15.

22. Consider, for example, how Shakespeare's impressions of the intensive preparations in England on the eve of the sailing of the Spanish Armada in 1588 get into his poetry some ten or more years later when Marcellus describes the day-and-night activity in Denmark (Hamlet I i 70–9).

23. In the National Library chapter of *Ulysses*.

24. *As You Like It* V iii 41.

25. *As You Like It* IV ii and V iii.

26. *A You Like It* III iii 32. Cf. 'full of matter' II i 68. Contrast V iii 35–7: 'though there was no great matter in the ditty, yet the note was very untuneable' (Touchstone's scathing upset of the antithesis 'music though not matter' which we expected).

27. See G. Gregory Smith, *Elizabethan Critical Essays* Vol. II (London, O.U.P., 1904) 39.

28. Bullough, *Narrative and Dramatic Source*, II, 157.

29. *Aminta* and *Il Pastor Fido* were printed together, but Guarini's work first, in *Il Pastor Fido Tragicomedia pastorale di Battista Guarini* (London, Per Giovanni Volfeo a spese di Giacopo Castelvetri, 1591). Guarini's chorus comes on 170–2, Tasso's on 252–4, of this edition.

A Lytton Sells, *The Italian Influence in English Poetry* (London, Allen and Unwin, 1955) 215, writes: 'So great at the time was the demand for the new pastoral poems that Castelvetro had the *Aminta* and the *Pastor Fido* printed at his own expense and . . . these easily accessible London editions encouraged the vogue of pastoral poetry which flourished in the 1590's . . .'

Sells gives a brief, vivacious glimpse of Guarini at the first performance of *Aminta*.

30. *The Countesse of Pembrokes Yuychurch* (London, Thomas Orwyn for William Ponsonby, 1591).
31. Under the title 'A Pastorall' this is the closing poem of the closing section – the 'Delia' section – of the *Works* of Samuel Daniel (London [V. Sims] for Simon Waterson, 1601). It is again printed as 'A Pastorall' in Daniel's *Certaine Small Poems Lately Printed* (London, G. Eld for Simon Waterson, 1605). E. K. Chambers has reprinted it in *The Oxford Book of Sixteenth-Century Verse* 535–7. Chambers has not reprinted Fraunce's version – but very few editors (with the exception of Yeats, who saw and proclaimed the charm of Spenser's Iambicum Trimetrum) have seen the living poetry in some of the quantitative experiments of the sixteenth century.
32. *As You Like It* I i 124–5.
33. In *Comparative Literature* (University of Oregon, Eugene, Oregon) Vol. XII, No. I, 348.

CHAPTER V

1. *Twelfth Night* II iv 33–6.
2. *Twelfth Nigh* V i 330.
3. *King Lear* V iii 220–1.
4. *Twelfth Night* I v 231 ff.
5. *Twelfth Night* II ii 22.
6. *Twelfth Night* II i 46–9.
7. *Twelfth Night* V i 135–6.
8. *Twelfth Night* I v 298 ff.
9. *Twelfth Night* III i 102–176.
10. *Twelfth Night* IV i.
11. See e.g. *The Shakespeare Allusion-Book*, re-edited John Munro, Vol. I (London, O.U.P., reprinted 1932) 457.
12. *Twelfth Night* I v 77–82.
13. *Twelfth Night* V i 297 ff.
14. *The Merchant* II v 52–5.
15. *The Case is Alterd*, II i 62–6. In Jonson, *Works*, ed. Herford and Simpson, Vol. II (Oxford, Clarendon Press, 1927).
16. *The Case is Alterd* III i 11–15
17. *Every Man Out of his Humour* I iii 60–2. In Jonson, *Works*, ed. Herford and Simpson, Vol. III.
18. *The Merchant* II i 193–208.
19. *Hassan* (London. Heinemann, Drama Library edition, 1951) 46.
20. *Works*, ed. Herford and Simpson, Vol. III, 598.
21. So reports Leonard Digges in the poem cited above.

NOTES

22. *Volpone* III vii 133–266. In Jonson, *Works*, ed. Herford and Simpson, Vol. V, 81–5.
23. Cf. *Works*, ed. Herford and Simpson, Vol. I, 18.
24. *Henry V* III ii 5–7.
25. *Henry V* IV i 84–5.
26. *All's Well* II iii 291–2.
27. *The Case is Alterd* II vii 75.
28. T. Dekker, *Satiromastix* II ii 77. In e.g. Jonson's *Poetaster* and Dekker's *Satiromastix*, ed. J. H. Penniman (Boston, Heath, 1913) 314.
29. See *Every Man in his Humour.*
30. On these grounds Samuel Johnson blames Shakespeare for ridiculing Andrew Ague-Cheek. Among his remarks at the tail of *Twelfth Night* he writes: '*Ague-Cheek* is drawn with great propriety, but his character is, in great measure, that of natural fatuity, and is therefor not the proper prey of a satirist.' Whereas, he continues, 'the soliloquy of Malvolio is truly comick; he is betrayed to ridicule merely by his pride . . .'
31. *Twelfth Night* II v 9.
32. *Twelfth Night* II viii 288.
33. *Twelfth Night* V i 377; 388.
34. *Twelfth Night* IV iii 16–20.
35. *The Silent Woman* V i 89–91. Jonson, *Works*, ed. Herford and Simpson, Vol. V.
36. *The Silent Woman* V iv 247.
37. I am of course omitting, only because it is so perfectly clear, another 'complication', which radically separates Shakespeare's scene from Jonson's: the pathos and sentiment that depend on our knowledge that Viola is a girl: 'A little thing would make me tell them how much I lack of man.' Jonson cannot equal Shakespeare in this kind of effect, and therefore avoids it. For him, total ruthlessness.
38. See e.g. *Essays of John Dryden*, ed. W. P. Ker, Vol. I (Oxford, Clarendon Press, 1900) 86.
39. Milton, *Paradise Lost*, I 502.
40. *The Merchant* V i 129.
41. Jonson, *Works*, ed. Herford and Simpson, Vol. I, 32.
42. Herford and Simpson, Vol. I, 141.
43. *The Case is Alterd* V viii 1–41.
44. *Volpone* III vii 139–267.
45. *All's Well* II i 173–6 (and her earlier conversation I i 121–80).
46. Cf. the last line of the Prologue to *Every Man In*: in *Works*, ed. Herford and Simpson, Vol. III, 303.
47. *A Midsummer Night's Dream* III ii 115.
48. *As You Like It* III iv 82.

NOTES

CHAPTER VI

1. E. K. Chambers, *William Shakespeare* (London, O.U.P., 1930) Vol. I, 76; Vol. II, 72.
2. Chambers, Vol. II, 329.
3. My quotations are from C. H. McIlwain's text in *Political Works of James I* (Cambridge, Mass., 1918). He followed the 1616 edition. I have checked the quotations against a 1603 edition (London, Felix Kyngston for Iohn Norton) and have found no discrepancies—in the passages I cite—other than minor differences of spelling. In the references below I give the pages of the 1603 edition for those who would like to see the passages as they looked at the crucial date.
4. (1603) 90.
5. (1603) 30–1.
6. (1603) 73–4.
7. A text is printed by Geoffrey Bullough, *Narrative and Dramatic Sources of Shakespeare*, Vol. II (London, Routledge and Kegan Paul, 1958) 442–513.
8. *Measure for Measure* III ii 423.
9. *Measure for Measure* II ii 91–102.
10. *Measure for Measure* V i 2.
11. Bullough Vol. II, 463.
12. Vol. II, 408.
13. *Measure for Measure* IV iii 139–40.
14. *Measure for Measure* V i 439–41.
15. *Measure for Measure* III i 86–7.
16. *Measure for Measure* III i 140–3.
17. *3 Henry VI* II i 42.
18. Stanzas 8 and 9. See e.g. Skelton, *Complete Poems*, ed. P. Henderson (London, Dent, 1948) 289.
19. *All's Well* V ii 57–8.
20. See e.g. Lucy Aiken, *Memoirs of the Court of James I* (Boston, 1822) Vol. I, 85.
21. See Arthur Cayley, *Life of Sir Walter Ralegh* (London, 1805) Vol. II, 4 ff.; Irvin Anthony, *Ralegh and his World* (N.Y., Scribners, 1934) 237 ff.
22. *Measure for Measure* I ii 165–6.
23. E.g. *Measure for Measure* III ii 124 ff. and IV iii 163 ff.
24. Cf. *Basilikon Doron* (1603) 52: 'But vnto one fault is all the common people of the kingdome subiect, as well burgh as land, which is, to iudge and speake rashly of their Prince . . .' And James goes on '. . . rule, as may iustly stoppe their mouthes, from all such idle and vnreuerent speeches . . .'

25. *Measure for Measure* III ii 196–9.
26. *Measure for Measure* III ii 273 ff.
27. *Basilikon Doron* (1603) 84. The marginal title to the passage in Kyngston's 1603 edition reads 'The right use of temperance'.
28. *Measure for Measure* V i 374.
29. *Measure for Measure* IV i 14–5.
30. Induction to *Bartholomew Fair*. In Jonson, *Works* ed. Herford and Simpson, Vol. IV, 16.
31. 'The Lepanto of James the Sixt', 10, in *His Maiesties Poeticall Exercises at vacant houres* (Edinburgh, Robert Walde-graue, n.d. [1591]).
32. *Measure for Measure* IV iii 41–73.
33. *Measure for Measure* II iii.
34. *Troilus and Cressida* II ii 97 ff.
35. *Measure for Measure* IV iii 163–5.
36. See e.g. H. Howarth and I. Shukrallah, *Images from the Arab World* (London, Pilot Press, 1944) 82.
37. *Measure for Measure* III i 136 ff.
38. *Measure for Measure* III ii 275–96.
39. *Measure for Measure* V i 374–5.
40. J. H. Newman, *The Dream of Gerontius*, 860.
41. *Measure for Measure* V i 448 ff.

CHAPTER VII

1. 'When did a Renaissance man grow old?', in *Studies in the Renaissance*, Vol. XIV (New York, Renaissance Society of America, 1967), 7–42.
2. *Winter's Tale* I ii 74–5.
3. Cf. *Henry VIII* II iv 236.
4. *Henry VIII* I i 157 ff.
5. *Henry VIII* I ii 18 ff.
6. *Henry VIII* I ii 105–7.
7. *Henry VIII* II ii.
8. For the Stratford, Ontario, performance of 1961 Leo Ciceri's agreeable features were rebuilt and coloured to suggest malignancy.
9. *Love's Labour's Lost* V i 27.
10. In *The Schoolemaster* (London, 1570). See e.g. G. Gregory Smith, *Elizabethan Critical Essays* Vol. I (London, O.U.P., 1904) 28.
11. *Lear* IV vi 128–9.
12. *Love's Labour's Lost* IV i 78.
13. *Measure for Measure* V i 444.
14. *Tempest* I ii 417–9.

15. *Tempest* V i 182–3.
16. *Tempest* IV i 189.
17. *Henry VIII* III i 145.
18. *Remaines of a Greater Worke, concerning Britaine* (London, G. Eld for Simon Waterson, 1605) 9–10.
19. *Henry VIII* III i 145.
20. *Henry VIII* III ii 371–2.
21. See e.g. C. M. Ingleby, *Shakespeare's Centurie of Prayse* (London, New Shakespere Society, Series IV, No. 2 Second ed. 1879) 125.
22. *Measure for Measure* III ii 245–6.
23. *Tempest* V i 208–13.
24. *Henry VIII* II ii 22 ff.
25. *Henry VIII* III ii 376 ff.
26. *Henry VIII* IV ii 64–5.
27. *Henry VIII* III ii 412 ff.
28. 'The Prologue for the Stage', Jonson, *Works*, ed. Herford and Simpson, Vol. VI, 282. And cf. Yeats, *Letters*, ed. Allan Wade (London, 1954) 465–6.
29. 'My Picture Left in Scotland', in e.g. *Poems of Ben Jonson*, ed. G. B. Johnston (London, Routledge, 1954) 127–8.
30. 'The Voice Alone', written for the twenty-fifth anniversary of the B.B.C.
31. *Richard III* III v stage directions.
32. In e.g. *The Shakespeare Allusion-Book*, re-edited John Munro, Vol. I (London, O.U.P., 1932) 239.
33. *Cymbeline* V iv 30–113.
34. *Cymbeline* III ii 54–61.
35. *Cymbeline* V v 183 ff.
36. *Henry VIII* V iii 130 ff.
37. *Henry VIII* IV i 88–9.
38. *Cymbeline* V iii 52.
39. *Pericles* V ii 33–4.
40. *Tempest* I ii 408.
41. See e.g. Coleridge, *Select Poetry and Prose*, ed. S. Potter (London, Nonesuch, 1933) 404–5.
42. *Henry VIII* V i 147–8.
43. *Henry VIII* IV ii 29–30.
44. *Winter's Tale* III ii 164–6.
45. *Winter's Tale* IV ii 60–1.
46. *Antony and Cleopatra* II ii 196 ff.
47. *Antony and Cleopatra* I iv 56 ff.
48. *Henry VIII* IV i and IV ii.

NOTES

CHAPTER VIII

1. (London, Bowes and Bowes, 1958.)
2. *Macbeth* IV iii 138–9.
3. *Richard III* V v 23 ff.
4. *Lear* III iv 32–3.
5. A. A. Mendilow and Alice Shalvi, *The World and Art of Shakespeare* (Jerusalem and New York, 1967) 215.
6. Francisco Lopez de Gómara, *Annals of the Emperor Charles V*, Spanish text and English translation, ed. Roger Bigelow Merriman (Oxford, Clarendon Press, 1912) 270.
7. See e.g. *History of Charles the Vth* of D. F. Prudencio de Sandoval, 'made English By Capt. John Stevens' (London, R. Smith, 1703). On the title-page the stages of Charles' life are set out, concluding '*Lastly*, Of the most Heroick Action of that Emperor's Life, his voluntary resigning up all his vast Dominions, and retiring to a Monastery'.
8. *Lear* III vii 73–5.
9. *Lear* I i 149–51.
10. See e.g. H. Howarth and I. Shukrallah, *Images from the Arab World* (London, Pilot Press, 1944) 35.
11. (London, Chatto and Windus, 1944) 85–6, 119.
12. *Op. cit.*, 225.
13. *Lear* V iii 313–15.
14. (except for her farewell to her 'kind lord') *Othello* V ii 122–4.
15. *Hamlet* V ii 359.
16. *Heraclides* 657–61.
17. 'with such ferret and such fiery eyes' *Julius Caesar* I ii 186.
18. In his marvellous essay, 'Love's Labour's Won', in *Shakespeare's Sonnets Dated* (London, Hart-Davis, 1949).
19. *Shakespeare's History Plays* 266.
20. In his *Complete Works of Shakespeare* (Chicago, Scott, Foresman, 1951) 726.
21. *Shakespeare's History Plays* 144.
22. 1 *Henry IV* II ii 90.
23. *Antony and Cleopatra* II vi 17.
24. 1 *Henry IV* III i 231.
25. *Shakespeare's History Plays* 309.
26. *Paradise Lost* IV 830.
27. *The Merchant of Venice* V i 58 ff.
28. Line 45 of the first chorus of *The Dog beneath the Skin* (London Faber, 1935) 13.
29. Especially *Hamlet* III ii 76–8.
30. *All's Well* I ii 69.

31. In *Shakespeare's History Plays* 66.
32. Shalvi and Mendilow *op. cit.*, 232.
33. *Shakespeare's Professional Skills* (Cambridge, C.U.P., 1964).
34. *Richard III* IV iv 148–50.
35. *Lear* V iii 184.
36. *Henry VIII* III i 3 ff.
37. *Lycidas* 58–63.
38. *Paradise Lost* VII 35–8.
39. *Hamlet* III iv 152.

Index

Index

Titles of plays by Shakespeare are listed
under 'Shakespeare'; titles of plays by
Ben Jonson under 'Jonson'

INDEX

Roman spirit 54
Rostand, E. 110, 154

Sannazaro 89
Sargent, R. M. 79
Schools 25
Sermons 33, 157, 180
Shaaber, Matthias 42
Shakespeare, Ann Hathaway
(Shakespeare's wife) 87
Shakespeare, John (Shakespeare's
father) 2, 6
Shakespeare, Mary Arden
(Shakespeare's mother) 18 (cf.
88)
Shakespeare, Susanna (Shakespeare's elder daughter) 40
Shakespeare, William: canniness
82; does several things concurrently in one scene 51, 83,
133, 138, 146; extends his
actors' vocal range 22–3; eye-
scenes alternating with ear-
scenes 158, 163–4; focus on
daughters 53, 129; heaps up
motives 56; likes to weigh pros
and cons 11–12; refines 22, 91;
scrutinizing mind 82; short
scenes to break up long scenes
138; snob 21; a sort of Jacob
59; a sort of Socrates 124,
154–6; trade-unionist 79–82
All's Well that Ends Well
15–16, 98, 109, 118, 130, 143,
180, 184
Antony and Cleopatra 23,
80, 143, 163, 166, 180, 189
As You Like It 18, 78–93,
94, 119, 120
Comedy of Errors 41, 43, 94,
102
Coriolanus 16–19, 38, 162,
169
Cymbeline 21–2, 159, 160,
161, 175

Hamlet 12, 14, 22, 27, 56,
63–77, 130, 166, 175, 184,
186, 191, 192–3 (Note 16),
197 (Note 22)
Henry IV: (both Parts) 13,
35, 41, 106–8, 144–5, 162,
166, 186; (Part I) 13, 143,
163, 166, 180–1; (Part II)
36, 178–9
Henry V 35–7, 108–9, 181
Henry VI: (all Parts) 31–4,
41, 116, 168; (Part I) 31;
(Part II) 31–2, 39, 40, 41, 43,
180; (Part III) 32, 41, 129
Henry VIII 20, 21, 143–64,
190
Julius Caesar 14, 43, 163,
166, 176, 178, 181
King John 3, 13, 26, 32
King Lear 41, 77, 95, 116,
129, 149, 155, 168–73, 175,
186, 189
Love's Labour's Lost 42, 77,
116, 149–50, 154, 158, 162
Macbeth 116, 135, 166, 167
168, 187
Measure for Measure 120–
142, 146, 150, 155
Merchant of Venice 8–9, 41,
45–63, 64, 72, 94, 103–5,
146, 158, 169, 183
Midsummer Night's Dream
7, 25, 45, 50, 61, 88, 94, 102,
119, 146, 158
Much Ado about Nothing
10–12, 14, 52, 103
Othello 14, 56, 136–7, 162,
166, 173–5, 189
Pericles 20, 21, 159, 161
Rape of Lucrece 6 (cf. 65)
Richard II 26, 35, 38, 40,
154, 166–7, 169, 171
Richard III 34, 40, 158,
162, 167, 188